P9-DDS-957

The Putt at the End of the World

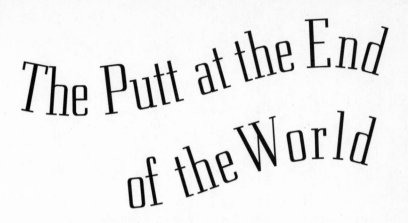

The Putt at the End of the World

A NOVEL BY

Lee K. Abbott, Dave Barry, Richard Bausch,

James Crumley, James W. Hall,

Tami Hoag, Tim O'Brien, Ridley Pearson,

and Les Standiford

Compiled and edited by Les Standiford

WARNER BOOKS

A Time Warner Company

This is a work of fiction. All of the characters, incidents, and dialogue, except for incidental references to public figures, products, or services, are imaginary and are not intended to refer to any living persons or to disparage any company's products or services.

Compilation copyright © 2000 by Les Standiford
Chapter One, Deep Rough, Copyright © 2000 by Les Standiford
Chapter Two, Blasting Out, Copyright © 2000 by Ridley Pearson
Chapter Three, Hung Up on the Lip, Copyright © 2000 by Tami Hoag
Chapter Four, Never Up, Never In, Copyright © 2000 by Lee K. Abbott
Chapter Five, Tight Lies, Copyright © 2000 by Tim O'Brien
Chapter Six, Immovable Obstructions, Copyright © 2000 by Richard Bausch
Chapter Seven, Free Drop, Copyright © 2000 by Dave Barry
Chapter Eight, Digital Pronation, Copyright © 2000 by James W. Hall
Chapter Nine, Right into the Heart of the Cup, Copyright © 2000 by James Crumley
Epilogue, Curse of the Nineteenth Hole, Copyright © 2000 by Anonymous
All rights reserved.

Warner Books, Inc., 1271 Avenue of the Americas, New York, NY 10020
Visit our Web site at www.twbookmark.com

 A Time Warner Company

Printed in the United States of America
First Printing: May 2000
10 9 8 7 6 5 4 3 2 1

Library of Congress Cataloging-in-Publication Data

The putt at the end of the world / Lee K. Abbott . . . [et al.].
   p. cm.
   ISBN 0-446-52600-2
    1. Golf—Tournaments—Scotland—Fiction.   I. Abbott, Lee K.
   PS3550.A1 P88 2000
   —dc21

                                           99-089030

Book design by Giorgetta Bell McRee

This book is dedicated to the good Doctor Golf himself.

With a very special thanks from all the inmates to Rob McMahon, who saw to it that we received our medications promptly, and to Scott Waxman, who arranged the occasional evening pass away from the home. We couldn't have done it without you.

CONTENTS

The Putt at the End of the World

... from the very moment your caddie removes your club cover and tees up your ball, through the address, the waggle, the take away, the impact and on up to the end of your swing and even on through to that splendid moment when you give your caddie a friendly whack with your club handle across his shoulders to set him off down the middle of the fairway, you will be as close to nirvana and perfection as any man has a right to be.

My hat is off to you. I can say no more.

—WILLIAM PRICE FOX, *Doctor Golf*

Chapter One

DEEP ROUGH

by Les Standiford

Redfish Key, Florida

"You see that one, Hector?" Alfonzo Zamora called, the squat, stocky form familiar to a generation of golfing fans outlined against the setting sun. He had his eyes screwed tight, squinting down the narrow tunnel of mangroves and palms guarding the brutal eighteenth hole of the Links at Redfish Key.

On toward 7 P.M. of a languid Florida summer evening, the light failing, the shadows murderous, anyone could be forgiven for losing sight of something as tiny as a golf ball, Zamora told himself. His belly was no more formidable than it had been when he'd waded across the Rio Grande from Santa Teresa to El Paso almost forty years before, and his drives were very nearly the equal of those he could hit back then, but, admittedly, his eyes were not the same.

"I saw where it came down," his longtime caddy said.

"Good," Zamora said, turning to hand over his driver.

"I dunno about *that*," big Hector said as he accepted the club.

"What are you talking about?" Zamora was already off the tee, moving toward their cart, anxious to get things over with. His opponent—one Harvey Byers, a bond trader from Palm Beach who had put up twenty thousand dollars for the privilege of playing eighteen holes with the legendary Marvelous Mex this day—was venturing out onto the members tee box a hundred yards or so ahead, waggling his club, readying himself for his own final tee shot.

Hector shrugged. He stowed the driver into the cavernous tooled leather bag that had once been given to Zamora by the president of the state of Chihuahua, then slipped on one of the head covers done up to resemble a tiny sombrero. "That water really sucks up," the caddy said. "That's what I'm talking about."

Zamora swiveled around, stared back down the fairway. The blue of the sky had paled; a bank of distant thunderheads had taken on a pinkish cast. A late breeze off the water stirred the overhanging palms. "No way," he protested. "I hit that ball good."

"You did hit it good," Hector said. He glanced at the little dog-eared yardage book he carried in the pocket of his T-shirt. "I'd say two-eighty, two-ninety, right into that lake on the left side of the fairway."

"What lake?" Zamora demanded.

"That one right down there," Hector said, pointing.

2

They had always been something of a Mutt and Jeff act, but the big man was truly losing patience with him, Zamora thought. One of the inevitable drawbacks to a long-term relationship. He'd been with Hector for almost thirty years, had run through four marriages in the same length of time.

Zamora stared. A long line of trees bordered the fairway, which seemed to widen out into a blue-green plain, just about where Hector's dusky finger was aimed. "That looks like grass to me," he said.

"Well now, that's the problem, isn't it?"

"Shit," Zamora said.

The solid crack of Byers's tee shot drifted back toward them.

"Watch for a splash," Zamora said, hopefully. "You seem to be good at it."

"*Ain't* splashin'," Hector said, peering off into the gloom. "That white man just split himself the middle."

Zamora sighed. "Come on, Hector, get in the cart."

Hector gave him a look. The caddy stood well over six feet, weighed somewhere between two-seventy-five and anybody's guess. He shouldered the heavy bag as if it were nothing but a day player's canvas tote and started off down the fairway. "I been carrying this bag for thirty years, I ain't about to turn it over to some machine at this stage of the game."

Zamora sighed again, then pressed the accelerator, heading toward what he'd just learned was a lake.

"Well, at least we didn't *lose* any money," Zamora was saying. He'd had to hurry to his cart and floor it to catch up with Hector as the caddy stalked off the eighteenth green. One into the lake, drop with a penalty, he'd been hitting three into the green. But he'd been a little long with that approach shot, had to settle for a two-putt, had finished with a five. The bond trader, meanwhile, had somehow managed a bogey as well, his lowest score of the afternoon, and, with the stroke Zamora had given him, had won the hole outright.

"Mmmm-hmmm," Hector said. His lips were tight, his gaze fixed on that bank of thunderheads in the distance. Big roiling bank of thunderheads—pink on top, dark blue on the bottom, some kind of silent lightning flashing around in between—it looked like a giant brain about to explode, Zamora thought.

"I mean, who wouldn't have taken that press? You got to make life interesting, Hector, or what the hell's the point?" Zamora persisted. "Double or nothing, guy hasn't hit one out of his shadow all day . . ."

Hector gave him a sidelong glance. "Was a time," he said, "when you were known for the same damn thing: take on a man with a full set of clubs and you with nothing but a taped-up Coke bottle—"

"Pepsi," Zamora corrected him.

Hector shrugged. "Same thing."

Zamora glanced back toward the green where Harvey Byers was peeling bills off a roll, handing them over to his own caddy. "You think he set me up?"

Hector made a snorting sound that might have been intended as a laugh. "You better start wearing those

4

glasses like the doctor said, Z-man. That's all I got to say. You seem to be missing quite a bit these days."

At that, Zamora turned his broad, bronzed Aztec features away, wondering what Hector would say if he told him he *had* been wearing glasses, contacts anyway. He'd slipped away to find a Specs-Is-Us outlet during that rain-out day at the Atlanta Senior Classic, had himself fitted for a pair of the soft lenses. And they'd worked fine, for a month or so. But now . . . He shook his head. The truth was, he didn't know what was happening with his eyes. Soon as he got back home, he'd go see the doctor again—

"Look out!" Hector cried, and Zamora came back with a start. He slammed on the brake of the cart, locking it into a power slide that stopped a few inches short of a decorative pond occupying the grounds between the clubhouse path and the parking lot. Vague orange shapes slithered around in the shallow water there—those giant Japanese goldfish, Zamora thought; either that or orange alligators. He reached down to the transmission lever, flipped the cart into reverse.

"Throw those clubs on the cart and get in," he said to Hector. "We got a plane to catch." Zamora had his foot poised atop the accelerator, was doing his best to ignore the shrill warning ping that the cart was sending out. He didn't have to read his watch to know they'd be cutting it close. Maybe forty-five minutes to make the last plane out; he was due in Orlando for an 8 A.M. tee time, a corporate outing with some executives from Disney the day before some new Senior event—the Mickey and Minnie Open.

Only ten grand for the outing, but he had alimony payments rolling around, and he'd just blown *this* appearance money. The way he'd been playing on the tour this season, it might be the only cash he could count on taking home from the Florida swing.

"I been meaning to talk to you about Orlando," Hector was saying. He had his head hanging down, the big bag off his shoulder now, resting it on the ground in front of him. He was moving from one foot to the other as if he might be practicing how to dance.

"Talk about what?" Zamora said. "We'll have plenty of time on the plane, man. Come on."

Hector glanced up finally. "Fact is, I won't be going to Orlando."

Zamora stared at him dumbly. He reached down, twisted the key of the cart. Though the pinging stopped, the throbbing at his temples did not. "You're not going to Orlando? Why the hell not?"

Hector rolled his big head around uncomfortably, glanced back in the direction of the eighteenth green. "Z-man, you don't have to make this any harder than it is."

"You sound like my last wife, Hector. Now tell me what's wrong."

"Well, you know we ain't been doing so well lately—"

"Don't tell me Hale Irwin's been after you again. Promising you things? I told you that guy is just trying to mess with me. He don't care about you, Hector, not like I do. Besides, he's picked up a hitch in his swing, and his putting stroke is shot. He lost back-to-back playoffs against a couple of nobodies."

Hector held up his big paw. "It's not Hale Irwin," he said sorrowfully. "I just told you I ain't going to Orlando."

"Well, *what* then?"

Hector shrugged, glanced back along the path toward the green. Harvey Byers, the bond trader, was striding their way, his smile glinting even in the fading light. "I got kids in high school, Z-man," Hector said. "About to go off to college. I got to be thinking of the future."

"Mr. Zamora," the bond trader was calling. "I wanted to catch you before you got away—"

"We're having a conversation," Zamora snapped.

"I better just leave these here," Hector said. He stepped forward, propped the big bag against the seat of the cart.

"Why don't you just go on inside, tell them you're with me," the bond trader said to Hector.

Zamora stared at Byers, then back at Hector. His mouth fell open as it began to dawn on him. "Hector!" he called. "Are you shitting me?"

But Hector didn't turn. He was moving down the path toward the clubhouse as quickly as Zamora had ever seen him move. Zamora swung back to Byers, who held his hands up in a placating manner.

"Now I know you must be upset . . . ," Byers began.

"Did you just hire my caddy away?" Zamora said. He vaulted over the clubs Hector had dumped in his path, and in one smooth motion had a handful of Byers's shirtfront before the man could step away.

"Hustle me out of twenty thousand dollars, steal my caddy . . ." Zamora dragged Byers toward the pond, had one hand on his collar, another at the seat of his pants. Yes, let them be orange alligators, he thought.

"Two hundred and fifty thousand dollars!" Byers cried, as Zamora neared the top of his backswing.

Zamora hesitated, glanced down at the man he held in

7

his hands. "You offered Hector that kind of money? He's a good caddy, but he's not that good."

"I'm offering *you* two hundred and fifty thousand dollars," Byers said. His voice sounded a little strange. "That's what I wanted to talk to you about."

Zamora realized he was strangling the man with his polo shirt. He released his hold on the back of Byers's collar. The man managed to catch himself on his palms, keep his face from smacking the curb at the edge of the pond.

"Are you going to let go of my pants now?" Byers asked. He looked like he was frozen halfway through a push-up.

"Maybe," Zamora said. One good sling and he could still run the man right into the water. "It depends on just how good this story is."

"It's not a story at all," Byers said. "It's true. It's why we brought you down here to begin with. We wanted to be sure your skills were still intact, you see, and they were outstanding, I must say, except for that final hole—"

"I *am* going to feed you to the fish," Zamora said. He noted agitated splashing in the pool now. Perhaps they were golden piranha. This was South Florida, after all.

"Please, Mr. Zamora, hear me out . . ."

"Just who is this *we*?" Zamora said, tensing himself for the toss.

"I represent Phillip Bates," Byers said.

"The computer guru," Zamora said, irony in his voice. "Richest man in the world."

"Not to mention golf aficionado," Byers added hastily. "Remember when he tried to buy Augusta Country Club?"

Zamora peered down through the gloom. Of course he

remembered. For what Bates had offered, even the supposedly inviolate membership of Augusta had finally caved in. It had taken an act of the Georgia legislature to keep the deal from going through. "What would Phillip Bates want from me?" he asked suspiciously.

Byers twisted his head around. In the gloom, only one eye visible, his mouth working awkwardly, he looked a bit like a fish himself. "He wants you to come to Scotland, Mr. Zamora."

"To Scotland?" Zamora said. He released his hold on Byers finally and the man dropped in a heap. "What the hell for?"

Byers got to his feet then, straightened his thinning blond hair, dusted his hands on his slacks. "For two hundred and fifty thousand dollars," he repeated, his voice back to something like normal. He had withdrawn his wallet, was holding out something that looked like a check. "Half to be paid now, half when the job is done."

"And what sort of job is this?" Zamora asked dubiously.

"Why don't we go inside and talk about it?" Byers said, handing over the check.

Zamora stared down. It looked like his name all right, and he thought all the zeros were in place. He checked the sky, saw he'd have to find better light to make sure the decimal point was right.

What the hey, he'd already missed his flight. He could go inside, do that much, he thought, and followed Byers away.

Palm Desert, California

Rita Shaughnessy stood beneath the patio overhang at the rear of the bungalow she had occupied for nearly a month at the Samantha Forbes Clinic, a copper-faced wedge poised about three-quarters back in her swing. Though it was a man's club, it hardly mattered. She'd been the longest-hitting woman on the tour, could outdrive more than a few of her male counterparts. Besides, she was hardly in a position to be picky about her equipment.

"Spend enough time in a place like this," she said over her shoulder, "you can figure out all sorts of things."

She hitched her hands just a bit higher. "One thing I realized, I'd been cupping my wrist at the top of my swing," she said. She gave a toss of her shoulder-length blond hair and, without appearing to look, brought the club down neatly onto the AstroTurf carpeting of the patio. The ball she'd placed there arced out into the clear desert sky, its white orb outlined cleanly against the purple range of mountains opposite.

The ball seemed to hang in the sky for an inordinate amount of time, and when it finally dropped, it landed with a gentle plop on the immaculately tended grass of the clinic's croquet court, took one quick hop backward, and came to rest by a wicket peg, not half a yard from where several other balls lay.

The croquet court was set like an emerald among the parched surroundings, had been carved into a gentle slope about fifty yards away, just this side of a pair of clay tennis courts and a sizable open-air pavilion where tai chi and stretching classes were conducted for those attempting to cleanse themselves during the cool morning hours.

"Maybe you ought to put some clothes on," Vin Baxter said, gesturing at an older couple who stood together under the pavilion roof, staring up their way.

"I *have* clothes on," Rita said.

"Not many," he said.

She gave him a smile. "You haven't been to the beach lately, have you?" In fact, she was wearing only a brassiere and bikini panties, and though Rita was not what anyone could call overweight, she was five foot ten and owned what her mother had once referred to as "certain bodily features." There was enough fabric in what she wore to make two or three outfits for any of the girls of *Baywatch*.

"I've been to the beach," he said, flushing slightly as she bent over another ball.

She smiled, and bent lower than was necessary toward the ball. She squeezed her arms together, gave an exaggerated waggle of the club just as Vin turned his gaze from her breasts toward the distant mountains.

Rita smiled to herself. Vin was her agent and business manager, but he was fairly new to the job. He was young—younger than she was, at least—and he would take time to break in. But unlike Nathaniel Phillips, her previous manager, Vin had not so far tried to tell her what to do. He had been content to couch his suggestions about what you might call her "exuberant" lifestyle in relatively deferential terms. This deference had a great deal to do with the fact that she was one of Vin's better-known clients, that despite her spotty earnings on the tour these past few years, there were few in the world of sports who

were unaware of the accomplishments of Rita Shaughnessy, both on and off the course.

And even though he hadn't much to show for all his
efforts on her behalf, Vin was eager and energetic, even
sincere at times. After all, he'd managed to get her into
this clinic, when the Betty Ford had declined to re-enroll
her after what had taken place during her fourth sojourn
there. Besides that, she thought, he was cute, in a Jerry
McGuire kind of way. It had been a while since she'd been
around a man whom she could make blush. That in itself
made him attractive.

"I had a call from the clinic director this morning," Vin
said, watching another shot soar out into the desert sky.

"You two *are* getting chummy," Rita said. She tipped
the half-empty range bucket on its side, flipped a ball to a
relatively unmarked spot on the chopped-up carpet with
the wedge blade.

"She's a bit concerned. She thinks you're backsliding."

"Nonsense," Rita said. She put a little something extra
into her downswing. There was a sharp report as the ball
hit the top of the pavilion, and the old couple ducked in
reflex.

She turned to him, hooked a finger to adjust a bra
strap. "The director's a twenty-four handicapper in a
scratch-event world. She's just upset about the cook."

Vin shook his head. "She didn't say anything about a
cook."

"The director of cuisine," Rita said. "That's his title.
He's really not such a bad guy, though. We made friends;
he comes up to the bungalow now and then, brings a little
cooking sherry along—"

"Jesus, Rita."

"He's the one who found me the clubs." She pointed to the eelskin bag leaning in the corner, a black monster that looked large enough to house a colony of bats. "Nicklaus left them here."

Vin stared. "Jack Nicklaus came to the Forbes?"

"My mistake," Rita said. "I meant Nicholson. The actor."

"Oh," Vin said.

The old couple had ventured a few steps out onto the gravel path that led from the pavilion toward the red-tile-roofed cluster of buildings that constituted the main compound of the clinic. Rita lobbed a pair of wedge shots in quick succession, and the balls smacked down into the sand, bracketing the pathway like mortar fire. The old couple yelped and scurried back under cover.

"Have you been drinking?" Vin asked.

"Is it five o'clock yet?"

"Ten past," he told her.

"There's your answer," she said.

"You promised you were going to buckle down, really work on things this time around, Rita. That's how I got them to agree to take you."

She turned to him, wide-eyed. "What do you call this?" she asked, sweeping her arm toward the neat circle of balls below. "Just watch." She brushed past him, close enough to send him into full-fledged blush, picked up an empty martini glass from the patio table. She walked out onto the strip of grass that abutted the bungalow and bent from the waist to settle the glass securely. She glanced back toward the patio through the inverted V of her legs, but Vin seemed to be examining his fingernails.

She came back to the patio, adopted a wide-open

stance, sent a flop shot in the direction of the glass. The ball landed a foot past the glass, bit hard, leapt backward. There was a tinkling sound as the ball settled into the conical bottom. She glanced up at him and grinned.

"Now *there's* a garnish," she said. "Two jiggers of vodka, splash of Rose's lime juice, add a Titleist 2. I'm still working on what to call it."

Vin glanced at the glass, then down toward the pavilion. The elderly couple had taken advantage of the moment, were hotfooting it up the path toward the main compound. Rita watched them for a moment, then turned back to him, a sorrowful expression on her face. "Some people have absolutely no sense of humor," she said.

Vin nodded, but he wasn't agreeing with anything. "You're going to have to leave here, Rita. That's what I came down to tell you."

She turned to stare at him. "Hey, Vin, I'm just having a little fun, that's all."

"They messengered in a refund check," he said. "And they've agreed not to say anything to the press so long as you just go quietly—"

"Geez, Vin, stop trying to sugarcoat it. How do they really feel about me here?"

"I assured the director we'd have you packed up and out before dark . . ."

Rita saw something in Vin's face, felt an unaccountable pang shoot through her. She'd had a sudden flash of the incident that had brought her to Forbes. Not halfway through the Jenny Jones Invitational in Santa Barbara, twenty-four strokes over par, at the dead bottom of the pack, a lock to miss her tenth cut in a row. She'd ducked into the ladies for a little pick-me-up toot, had dropped everything onto the floor. She'd been on her hands and knees in front of the toilet, snorting whatever looked right through a rolled-up twenty when Nancy Lopez had walked in on her. Rita had caught a glimpse of her stunned face before she whirled away, slamming the door in her wake.

She'd stood up, wiped the grime off her knees, smoothed her skirt, and walked out in the bright sunshine, then straight across the fairway and into the clubhouse bar. Someone had called Vin to come get her later that night. Much later. Good old Vin, she thought. She seemed to remember throwing up in his car.

She laid the wedge down across the patio table, took a step toward him. "Hey, I'm sorry, okay? I'll drop it in reverse a couple of notches, I promise . . ."

"It's too late, Rita."

"Come on, Vin. You're right. I need to work on things a little while. I'm not ready to go back out on tour, not just yet. A couple more weeks here, I can get it together—"

"Rita!"

She heard a note in his voice she never had before, enough to stop her. Stop her dead. She stared back at him.

So quiet here in the desert, she realized. In the distance, she could hear the sound of music. Mozart, most likely. They liked to pipe Mozart through the public area speakers just before dinnertime.

"Where am I going to go, Vin?" she said, hating the plaintive tone she heard in her own voice. "I sublet my place in Malibu. They blackballed me at Chateau Marmont, I got this huge tab at Sportsman's Lodge—"

He held up one hand like a traffic cop, was reaching into his coat pocket with the other. "You know me, Rita,

I'd never leave you flapping in the wind." He handed over an envelope.

"What's this?" she asked. She noticed her fingers were trembling as she took the paper.

He shrugged. "It's a kind of corporate thing—"

"Oh no, Vinnie. I told you, no more outings with the suits. I hate those assholes. They're all like Rodney Dangerfield, without the jokes—"

"You're not in a *position*," he cut in, and the chill in his tone stopped her again. He saw the look in her eyes and glanced away, softening his voice. "The money's good," he said. "Damned good, considering." He held up his hand to keep her from saying anything. "The best thing is, this one's out of the country. It'll get you out of the eye of the storm for a bit . . ."

"Out of the country? As in where?"

"Scotland," he told her.

"Scotland, huh. Who's the sponsor, Cutty Sark?"

"You wish," he told her dryly. "This is something Phillip Bates cooked up."

"Bates? The guy who owns Macrodyne Software?"

Vin shrugged. "They wouldn't let him in Augusta, he built his own course in Scotland." He pointed at the envelope. "It tells about it in there. He bought a castle, several hundred acres on the coast north of Edinburgh. Apparently, there was one hole there already, the earliest anyone's ever found. Bates added another seventeen. No one's ever played the course. No one's even *seen* it."

She opened the envelope, saw something flutter toward the carpet at their feet. She reached out, snatched the check in midair. She turned it over, checked the figure, looked up at Vin in surprise. "All this for a round of golf?" she said. "What else do I have to do?"

"Hey, the guy's made of money," he said. "And that's *after* my cut."

She took a breath then, tapping the check speculatively with a nail. "I dunno, Vin . . . all that way . . . and there's a lot of scotch in Scotland."

"There's a lot of scotch everywhere, Rita."

She nodded disconsolately. "Maybe you could come along?" Her voice rose hopefully.

"I wish I could," he told her. "But you'll have to handle this one on your own."

She glanced down at the check once more. She'd held bigger in her day. But she'd be hard pressed to remember just how long it had been. All that money that had come and gone. Would it have been any different if she'd gone into computer programming? she wondered.

"We can always tell them no," Vin was saying.

She glanced up at him, feeling the chill that always came to the desert about this time of day. She turned, picked up her robe from one of the patio chairs, wrapped it tightly around her. She reached and patted Vin's well-tanned cheek.

"Never mind that," she told him. And went to pack her things.

Squat Possum Golf Club,
near Cambridge, Ohio

"Lordy, what a shot," the man in the gimmee cap said, watching Billy Sprague's ball drift down toward the tiny green set in the valley floor far below. "It's going in."

"No it isn't," Sprague said calmly. He was tall and angular, with a certain resemblance to Jimmy Stewart, his voice carrying a similar down-home twang that lent an extra note of gravity to whatever he said. "It's going to hit about six feet past the pin, and stick."

There were four men in the group altogether, and they stood watching from an elevated tee, built on a ridge that had once been part of a strip-mining tract. When demand for soft coal had fallen sometime in the late forties, the strip mine had been abandoned, and the golf course constructed atop its somewhat softened contours. The project had been the brainchild of Earle "Doc" Toland, who'd picked up the land for a song and built the course despite the general disparagement of the surrounding community's business leaders, most of whom thought the site far more suited to become a bass-fishing lake, or perhaps a tire vulcanizing plant, maybe even the town dump.

Toland, however, was something of a visionary. He had traveled to Europe, studied medicine in faraway Cleveland, had seen such miraculous sights as department store escalators, soft-serve ice cream, and golf courses. When he had returned to his hometown to practice, he had brought with him not only some knowledge of the physical needs of his patients, but their spiritual needs as well. Thus it was not long before the vision of Squat Possum

18

Golf Club had taken shape in Toland's mind, and he had spent every spare dollar and every free moment away from the swabbing of strep throats and the delivering of squalling babies to see that the vision became reality.

Though Toland was certainly one of the area's most eligible bachelors, he never married, for his true passion was Squat Possum. From the initial stirrings of spring to the first day snow flew in winter, it was the same: nine holes in the mists of early morning, before his rounds at the county clinic, another nine in the fading light of evening, after he'd ducked away from his burgeoning family practice. In his younger days he reserved whole Saturday afternoons for a full eighteen, and Sundays for thirty-six, for even in those days the one permissible substitution a God-fearing man might make for a contemplative hour or two in church was that properly reverent walk through the natural sepulcher of golfdom.

In his later years Toland modified his routine, spending more time tending to the course itself, modifying and making improvements (a driving range, fairway bunkers, an irrigation system) to his initial design, as well as spending more and more time in the tutelage of youngsters who might carry on his passion once he was gone. And though Toland had been mentor to many a fine player in his day, had sent more than one lad off to college on the wings of a golf scholarship, none of his pupils had been more apt than the one who had just struck the ball this tender summer evening, and the name of that man was Sprague.

For a number of years Billy Sprague's name had been affixed to every trophy awarded in every amateur tournament held south of Akron and east of Cincinnati, and many more besides. He'd attended Ohio State University in Columbus, where he'd equaled or broken every record set by the great Golden Bear himself. And when he had girded up his loins and strode out upon the field of professional play a dozen years before, expectations of his success were boundless.

The man in the gimmee cap knew none of this, however, for he was from West Virginia, a man who had come to golf late, after a career in dragline operation and maintenance had finally provided him with the wherewithal to retire and pursue more leisurely interests. With much practice and great determination he had whittled his handicap down into the high teens, and had accepted this day at the invitation of a friend, Blaine Craig, the owner of a Cambridge trucking company, to join in a round of golf at Craig's home club of Squat Possum.

As it turned out, the foursome included Craig, his brother Tom, Billy Sprague, and Winston Park, former dragline operator. The Craig brothers were good, significantly better than Park, their scores just a few strokes over par as they stood on the tee box of the par-three fourteenth hole. Park had not done badly himself. He was holding it at even bogey, not bad for a strange course, and with the strokes the Craigs had given him, he was already feeling his wallet fatten.

It was Billy Sprague, however, who had dazzled them all. He had belted every tee shot straight enough to lay pipe to, lashed irons to every green in regulation, his swing equally effortless and well made, no matter what club he held. On the greens themselves he'd lipped out a putt or two, but not many. Though the bets had been arranged according to match play and the Craigs thus paid attention to what happened scorewise only hole by hole, Winston Park knew that Sprague, who had declined the invitation to join in the wagering, stood at least six under, and this with five holes left to play. He might have been a rank amateur, Park thought, but he knew enough to realize he was in the presence of greatness.

Right now, for instance, as he gazed down through the southeastern Ohio haze to the tiny green on the valley floor below, he was watching the whirling ball do exactly what Sprague said it would do, strike no more than six feet beyond the flag and stop dead.

"Man," Winston Park said, doffing his Weirton Steel hat and clapping it to his chest. "You are something else."

Sprague glanced up from retrieving his tee and gave Park his guileless smile. "Thanks," he said, as if he'd never heard such a compliment before. And then they were all off the tee.

"This guy is a *club* pro?" Park said to Blaine Craig a few minutes later. "*Your* club pro?"

Craig, who was driving the cart down the precipitous path toward the green below, glanced over casually. "You making some sort of comment about Squat Possum?"

"No, no, it's a nice little course," Park protested. "I mean, we still have sand greens down where I play." Park was wishing Craig would turn his attention back to the narrow roadway. "It's just that . . . well, he's really *good*. Even I can see that much."

Blaine Craig nodded, apparently appeased. "Twelve

years we've had him, ever since Doc Toland retired." He turned back, gave Winston Park an odd look. "Sprague is sumpin' all right." He took the cart around the last bend, gave it full out down the last straightaway, his normally vacuous expression turning thoughtful. As they were getting out of the cart, Craig nodded toward the green where his brother and Billy Sprague were already walking.

"I want you to watch something now," Craig told him.

"Watch what?" Park asked, puzzled.

"Just wait and see," Craig said enigmatically and went to whisper something in Billy Sprague's ear.

Winston Park never did find his ball in the scrub brush bordering the creek that ran left of the green and gave the course its name. After five fruitless minutes of searching, he had to take a drop, then skulled his chip shot well past the hole. He misjudged the speed of the green coming back and nearly sent his first putt into the opposite fringe. He managed a decent lag on his next attempt and Tom Craig conceded the short putt for a six. Tom and Blaine were already in at four, both having made lengthy putts to salvage bogey. Twenty dollars going the other way, Winston Park thought ruefully.

It fell to Billy Sprague, then, to finish up. He surveyed his putt for what seemed an uncharacteristic length of time, then stepped up, hitched at his pants a couple of times, glanced at Blaine Craig at least twice before he bent over the putt in earnest. Craig, meantime, seemed to have turned his attention on the swifts wheeling about in the dusk, the creatures feinting and diving after insects like giant commas finally set free from a page.

Something going on, Park thought, just as Sprague drew back to putt. Instead of the smooth stroke Park had come to expect, however, what came next was a palsied stab, a slashing movement that sent the ball screaming past the hole, all the way across the green, where it disappeared into the thick collar of the second cut.

Park stared in astonishment, but the Craig brothers idled about, apparently unconcerned, as Sprague went soundlessly after his ball. At the collar, Sprague didn't bother to change clubs. He steadied himself over a dark clump of grass, then swatted his putter down in a way that made Winston Park think of his own swing as fluid.

The ball careened on a wild diagonal out of the thick grass, finally wobbling to a halt some fifty feet away, near the front of the green. Sprague was looking at no one by this point. He strode to the front of the green, resumed his stance over the ball, drew back . . . and whistled this one so far beyond the hole that Winston Park had to use the flag he'd been tending for a balance point, do a little two-step to get out of the way.

"I think that's enough," Sprague called, his voice as untroubled as ever. "You can pick that up for me, if you don't mind."

Winston stared down at the ball, then back at Sprague, who was already following the Craig brothers off toward the nearby tee. What was going on? Park wondered. He was suddenly hesitant about picking up Billy Sprague's ball, but he told himself that was foolish and forced himself to snatch the thing up. The ball wasn't really glowing hot, Park told himself as he hurried away. But it sure seemed as if it were.

By the time Park caught up, the others were already on the fifteenth tee, a long par-four, according to the carved wooden marker that featured a colorful relief map of the dogleg ahead. The tee box was set into the side of a hill, with the back and right side fashioned into a bulkhead of railroad ties. The big things had been stacked up where the hillside had been cut away to prevent erosion onto the flat surface of the tee itself, but the effect was one of teeing off alongside the walls of a log cabin. The Craig brothers went off first, both of them managing decent, if undistinguished, efforts toward the fairway. Sprague turned to motion Winston Park forward, but Park shook his head.

"Hell no," he said, tossing Sprague his ball. "No way I'll ever take honors from you."

Sprague shrugged, snatched the ball deftly. As he bent to tee it up, Blaine Craig gave Park a knowing smile.

"You better watch yourself," he said softly.

"Why's that?" Park whispered back, just as Sprague swung, an awkward lunge that bore no resemblance to the graceful passes he'd made all the livelong day.

There was a terrific crack as Sprague's ball shot nearly sideways off the tee. It slammed into one of the heavy ties, then caromed sharply backward, narrowly missing Park and the Craig brothers as it disappeared down the hill in the direction of the meandering creek.

"Dear Lord," Winston Park said as he straightened. He had no idea what it must have felt like to watch Rome burn, of course, but the stirrings inside him at that moment could not have been greatly dissimilar.

"Sorry, guys," Sprague said. His face showed no hint of emotion. "Looks like I'm going to have to go in anyway." He juked his thumb over his shoulder. Down the fairway, Park saw a cart fast approaching. In contrast to the beige models the four of them were driving, this one was painted a dark color, with a Plexiglas windscreen glinting orange with the last rays of the sun. As the cart neared, Park saw that a narrow-shouldered black man in bib overalls was at the wheel, that no clubs were tethered at the back.

"Sorry if I let you down, Blaine," Sprague said. "But you ought to know better. Nice meeting you, Mr. Park. You come back anytime, you hear?"

Winston Park felt his hand wave of its own accord as Sprague conferred briefly with the driver of the black cart. In the next moment, Sprague was in the seat and gone, and Park had turned in disbelief to the Craigs. "What the hell did you say to him?" Park asked. "I never saw such a thing."

Blaine Craig and his brother shared a smile that turned into a laugh, then outright guffaws. "That's the thing about Sprague, you see," Blaine Craig said, when he finally managed to stop laughing. "He's the best that ever was, so far as anyone around here knows, anyhow."

"But . . ." Winston Park was still shaking his head in bewilderment. "It was like a switch flipped."

"It did," Tom Craig cut in, wiping at his eyes. "That's just it. That's why the guy bombed out on the Tour. So long as there's no money involved, Billy Sprague can play like the angels. But the minute you bet him a dime." He pointed at the nearby tee. "Well, you saw what happens."

Winston Park stared off down the darkening fairway in

the direction of the departing cart. "I still don't get it," he said to Blaine Craig. "If he knows it, why'd he accept your bet?"

Blaine shook his head. "I didn't bet him. I didn't have to. I just told him *you* laid a hundred with me, you wanted to take ten strokes and see if you could beat his score for the last five holes. That's all it took to throw him, just being the *subject* of a bet."

Winston Park digested the enormity of it for a moment. "Well," he said finally, "that seems kind of cruel then, what you did."

Blaine Craig considered this, staring off into the dusk and the whirling cloud of swifts. "Well I suppose it is," he said as a delicious leer crossed his face. "But ain't it a hell of a lot of fun to watch?"

"What do you mean the old man's sick?" Billy Sprague was saying as Teddy drove them resolutely through the gloom. "Did you call the doctor?"

"He didn't want the doctor," Teddy told him. "He said to get you."

"You shouldn't pay attention to that," Sprague said. "He's an old man." He wasn't one to make an outburst — and had long ago learned how to control those impulses that might have sent him into a rage at what had just happened with the Craigs and Winston Park, for instance — but for God's sakes, it was Doc Toland they were talking about now.

Teddy seemed unmoved. "He says get *you*, that's who I get."

"All right," Sprague told him. "Can't this thing go any faster?"

"Nope," Teddy said, arraying them on. "I told Doc, let's take the governor off your cart, but he says, 'Teddy, ever'body else has a governor on their cart, so we'll just have to live with one ourselves.'"

"You do him pretty well," Sprague said, his eyes on the maintenance building that was taking shape in the gloom up ahead.

"Ought to," Teddy said, allowing himself a rare smile. "Been listening to the man fifty years."

The cart bounced onto the rough gravel of the maintenance yard, crackling on toward the base of the old stone structure, its whitewashed face glowing unnaturally white in the last light. The building had originally housed the offices of the strip-mining operation, but Toland had pressed it into service as his clubhouse for Squat Possum's first couple of decades.

As the membership had grown and Doc's practice swelled, a new clubhouse had been erected on a promontory out near Byesville Road, a handsome glass and native fieldstone building that afforded a striking view of the rolling, hardwood-studded countryside. The old offices had been converted again, this time to a maintenance building, along with spartan residential quarters Doc Toland had rigged down in the basement rooms, where he could stay close to the place that he loved.

As a child visiting Doc's chambers, Billy had always found it a dank, almost subterranean place, more like a cave than somewhere for a person to live. But as he'd grown older he'd come to understand something of Doc's fondness for it.

Not such a bad place for an eccentric bachelor to tuck himself away, Sprague had come to understand, and at the same time felt an uncomfortable jolt, as if he might be envisioning dragging himself into the very same cave one day. There *were* certain unmistakable similarities between the two of them after all.

Though, unlike Doc, Sprague had once been married; the union had not long survived the aftermath of his colossal failure upon the Tour. The daughter of an Upper Arlington banker was not about to settle down as happy homemaker for the head professional of far-flung Squat Possum Country Club, and for that Sprague could not really blame her. Since Daisy, however, he had not found anyone—or perhaps, he thought, he simply had lost the heart for it, had turned his passions toward the one lover who never failed to give him all he might desire (or almost never), and that focus was what linked him, so to speak, most obviously with Doc.

Sprague had reached the bottom of the steps by now and turned to knock at the great wooden slab of a door, entered when he heard Doc's wheezy voice sound inside. From what Teddy had said, Sprague had expected to find the old man laid out in his bedroom. Instead, he was surprised to find him in the cluttered living room, propped up in the old leather recliner he often slept in these days. It was a battered old thing but comfortable, its footrest often raised, as now, in front of the stone fireplace where Teddy kept a fire banked against the perennial damp and chill of the place in all but the hottest months.

"How'd you hit 'em?" Toland wheezed, raising a hand in greeting as Sprague entered.

"A bit too often," Sprague said. "Especially toward the end."

"That happens," Toland said. "Even to the best."

Sprague nodded, his eyes adjusting to the dim light of the room. The old man had been failing in recent months, but it was something he didn't want to recognize he supposed. Something they all simply refused to see. Now, however . . . he shook his head. "Teddy told me you weren't feeling so hot," he said. "He said you wanted to see me." He stood regarding the old man for a moment longer. "I think we need to take you into town."

The old man waved his hand as if there were a bothersome fly at his face. "Forget about town," he said. He patted the arm of his chair. "You come over here. Sit yourself down."

Sprague hesitated. He was almost thirty-five, but old habits died hard. Doc Toland asked—or told—you to do something, you found yourself doing it. He'd never spoken sharply, never shown anything but a moment's disappointment at Sprague's numerous failings over the years, but still you just did what the man said.

He stepped over a pile of golf magazines, found his way to Toland's chair. The old man glanced down at the stack, gave a laugh that turned into a long, hacking cough. "They send me all that stuff," he managed finally, his eyes glistening. "Hundred ways to help your game." He shook his head wonderingly. "How to shine your sticks and *keep* 'em shined." He laughed at his own feeble joke.

"So how come you wanted to see me?" Sprague asked. He had an awful premonition. Doc Toland had summoned him for the final speech. *"All this will now be yours, my son . . ."*

Sprague's own parents were long dead. His father in an auto accident his senior year of college, his mother of a heart attack not long after. He got no more than an annual Christmas card from Daisy, who had remarried several years ago. Toland was all the family he had left.

"Got something in the mail today for you, too," the old man said. He paused to cough again, then reached for a heavy-looking envelope that lay on the fireplace platform at his side.

"What is it? Another invitation to a qualifier? You can just toss it right in there."

"Ah no," Toland said, pulling the envelope back from him. "You don't want to burn this one up, son."

"If it's about a golf tournament, I do."

"That's not exactly what we're talking about," the old man said.

"If there's money involved—"

"Just keep quiet a minute," Toland said, and the tone in his voice sent Sprague right back into eighth-grade yes-sir mode. "You ready to listen to me?"

"Sorry, Doc."

Toland nodded, but he was already past the moment, had something more important on his mind. "I met a man in Scotland once, when I was about your age, taught me a few things about the game."

"What does that have to do with—"

"Just quiet!" the old man said. He cleared his throat and began again. "We've kept in touch over the years, he and I, one thing and another, I told him about you, of course . . ."

"What about me?"

The old man glanced up, fixed him with a gaze. "That you were the best, son. The best I ever saw . . ."

"Let's not get into that again."

Toland waved that away. "This man knows about the thing with you and the money. But he needs you anyway."

Sprague shook his head. "Needs me for what?"

"What else? He needs you to play a round of golf, that's all."

"That's what this is about?" Sprague said. He was relieved, of course, but a little annoyed as well. He had another look at Toland. Where he'd seen frailty a few moments ago, he now saw strength, the canny gaze of a fox. So he was to give some wizened Scotsman a playing tour of Squat Possum, let the man see all of what Doc Toland had wrought. He sighed. What was all the fuss for? "When's your pal coming in?"

Toland shook his head. "You'll have to go to him, I'm afraid."

"Oh yeah, like to Scotland I suppose." Sprague was trying to keep the irony out of his voice.

Toland seemed almost agitated now. "That's it, son. That's exactly it."

Sprague was reaching his limit. He was tired and hungry and vaguely embarrassed about what had happened with the Craig brothers earlier. He wanted to trudge on up to the grill in the nice new clubhouse, have himself a beer or three, scarf down a burger, drag himself into town to bed.

"Now why would I want to go to Scotland just to play a round of golf with some guy I've never met?"

Doc Toland smiled and pulled himself up straighter in his chair at that. "To lift the curse, that's why."

"The curse?" Sprague glanced around the room, feeling his hackles rise. Clearly Teddy had been right after all. The old man needed help, and fast. "Just sit still, Doc, I'm going to bring my car around—"

But the old man seemed frantic, had lunged all the way out of his chair now. He staggered forward, thrusting the envelope toward Sprague. "You're going over there to save the world as we know it, son." And as Sprague felt the envelope come into his hands, the old man pitched onto his face and lay still.

Chapter Two

BLASTING OUT

by Ridley Pearson

The Roundtable, on the shores of Lake Washington, Seattle, Washington

Mired in controversy from its inception, the Roundtable, a staggering architectural accomplishment, perched out over the relatively tranquil waters of Lake Washington looking like a combination of a Frank Lloyd Wright and a Marriott Courtyard hotel. Its four acres of copper roof winking relentlessly at the downtown Seattle skyline, its one hundred and twenty-five west-facing windows gleaming squeaky clean in the noonday sun. Moderately mature trees would someday fill out and obscure a good deal of its facade, but for the time being anyone with a boat could view the entire monstrosity from just offshore. Larger and grander private residences existed in the world. Versailles came to mind. Maybe some palace in the Middle East no one had ever heard of. But even Ted Turner could not lay claim to the largest, most expensive private home in North America. That title belonged solely to Phillip Bates.

"Anyplace you want to be?" Bates said, standing in front of the living room wall with a small electronic remote in hand. "Just name it," he said to his guest and COO, Roger Felt.

Felt said, "Venice."

"Any particular hotel or address?"

"You're kidding, right?"

Bates answered with an impish grin. At thirty-nine, all the man lacked was pimples in order to complete the impression of a boy of eighteen. He wore a T-shirt and blue jeans, Air Jordans, and white Peds bearing the Nike logo. His voice, like Michael Jackson's, had never broken, but instead reminded the listener of a castrato. "I'll give you my favorite." What had appeared to be a window looking out on Lake Washington—complete with traffic on the floating bridge and a sailboat on the water—suddenly offered a menu of choices in its uppermost corner. Bates expertly surfed through the menu in a matter of seconds, explaining, "What you were actually looking at just now was a high-res video image of the live action outside. Looked pretty convincing, didn't it?" he said proudly. "HDTV eat your heart out!" He completed the work with the remote, his final click delivering an astounding view down Venice's main canal. The other six windows in the room also changed views simultaneously, each affording a different angle on the same spectacular Venetian cityscape. "I can give you midnight, sunset, sunrise—any time of day you want. And what's especially phenomenal is . . . Well, go ahead and step up to one of the windows and look outside."

Roger Felt hauled his graying, fiftyish, large-bellied self to one of the displays and gasped. "But . . . how is that possible?" He scurried to the next window. He could see the entire city, no matter which direction he looked.

"We've installed this in both the dining room and my bedroom in the castle," Bates crowed. "Wait till they get a load of this!"

"This is going to revolutionize interior design."

"Want a Rembrandt? A van Gogh? Just a click away. Any one of these windows will convince you you're in the Louvre."

"You know," Felt said, "for all the board meetings, all the number crunching, you don't really have any idea how cool this shit is until you see it in person."

"Twenty thousand and change, per window. Another five years, that'll fall to below ten. A decade from now, smaller units will be installed in mobile homes. Mark my words. We just changed the way the world relates to the environment. Basement office? No problemo. Tired of the power lines? Digitize them out of the picture and change your view. Live in Venice for a year. Your choice." He beamed. "That's why I love that new slogan: 'We Imagine Your World.' A play on words there: Reimagine your world. Right?"

Felt rarely disagreed with Bates. Not with those stock options lurking out there. Not with four teenagers lined up for college like jets for landing at O'Hare. "Right," he echoed.

Bates signaled Felt to follow him, and the two walked

out through teak French doors—real doors, not digital—
onto the top of five levels of deck that descended elegantly
toward the lake, Bates grabbing two putters from the
Ming Dynasty urn that he used as an umbrella stand.
Deck level two housed a lap pool, level three, courtyard
dining off the third of the home's three full kitchens, but
this top deck laid claim to a seven-hundred-square-foot
Bermuda grass putting green complete with a pin in the
hole, the flag of which bore the logo of the Bates software
empire. Bates dropped a ball, sighted the putt, and sank a
twenty-footer.

Felt had tried to learn the game for the sake of his corporate standing, but the lessons never really paid off. He
missed a five-foot putt and kicked the ball out to a greater
distance where missing would be more understandable.
He didn't mind the game so much. Hitting a white "duck
egg" around a manicured lawn wasn't so bad; it was the
time requirement that ate into him. Nine holes meant an
hour and a half to two hours of his life gone to trying to
sink a very small ball into a very small hole somewhere a
long way from where one started. Eighteen holes was
three hours or better. Bates played thirty-six holes most
Sundays and expected his executives to join him if he
couldn't drum up Michael Jordan or Jack Nicholson.
Nicholson, fresh out of a stay at the Samantha Forbes
Clinic, had shot a sixty-four their last round out together,
and Bates wasn't too fond of looking so bad. Nonetheless,
Jack was on the list for Scotland.

"Let's talk about Scotland for a minute," Bates said,
sinking another sixteen-footer. The guy was as good as the
Golden Bear on the greens. He sucked from the tees.

That was the other thing: Bates liked to do most of his

serious business on the golf course. It had started in a garage fifteen years ago. Then it was the conference room. Then it was the private 707. Now it was the third fairway. Felt attempted a twelve-footer and missed the hole by two feet. Bates looked over at him like he was from Mars.

"The board is firmly behind this Scotland thing," Felt said, immediately regretting his tone.

"'Thing'?" Bates quoted.

"This world conference, or whatever."

"It *is* a world conference."

"It's a weekend golf tournament, Phillip," Felt reminded. "One that is costing this company's shareholders twelve million dollars. I have no idea what you personally have into the facility. Twenty? Thirty? Eighty? Nor how much you are personally putting into this party. The airfare, the pro fees, the private train from London?"

"It's publicity. It's the launch of the new operating system. It's the opening of the course. It's a chance to make some real headway toward world peace. Do they have religion in common? Hell no. Economies? No. Women? Food? Cultures? No. But every one of these guys plays golf. Every one of them! Qaddafi, Arafat, Multzunu, our own president. You're thinking in terms of *dollars*, Roger? You've got to think bigger."

"Twelve million is an expensive party, Phillip."

"We get a million back for the network coverage of the last round. ESPN went half a million for the first two rounds. When all is said and done you're out ten million. That's like five spots on the Super Bowl, for Christ's sakes! You realize the bang for the buck we're getting here? We'll be on every front page around the world for three days. Every evening news report in seventy-three languages. I gave both NPR and the BBC suites in the castle. World leaders will be talking about this party for the next six months. Every time there's a goddamn G7 meeting, the first thing off their lips will be how much fun they had in Scotland. And that's *us*. That's brand identification, brand loyalty. It's cheap at twice the price." He dropped an eighteen-footer. The guy couldn't miss. In anything.

Ned Gorman's office cubicle sat between two women, both Special Agents, both of whom wore such different perfumes that just to breathe normally brought on fits of nausea. He had finally resorted to a small Brookstone fan that he'd clipped to the cubicle's only shelf and aimed back at his face like a mini-hurricane so that his fine and sparse hair danced around and tickled his worried forehead. At thirty-four, Gorman was not only the oldest field operative assigned to the counterterrorism squad—the most "senior," as it was politely termed—but was currently the only Caucasian. Hillary Rodriguez, to his right, she of the orange musk, was twenty-nine, single, and built like a brick shithouse. He had the luxury of looking at her body in profile most every day. Despite the two large moles beneath her lower lip, he wanted badly to ask her out, and for the last two years had been debating a line of attack to that end. Vicky Chew, to his left, of gardenia fame, looked like something from the cover of *Vogue*—petite, shapely, and head-spinningly gorgeous. Vicky claimed to be engaged, though Ned had never met her fiancé, and if true it was one of the longest-running engagements in marital history—approaching eighteen months now. Ned was guessing it was a ruse to keep suitors like himself from even thinking about it. Vicky tended to wear clingy clothing, silk mostly, and not much underneath it, so that most days she looked spray painted rather than dressed. Ned Gorman liked his job.

A total of six field operatives worked the FBI's counterterrorism desk in the new Washington Metropolitan Field Office building. Telephone work for the most part. Informants, international contacts, computer hackers, and the Bureau's own diplomatically immune adjuncts who were legally attached to various embassies throughout the world. When Ned Gorman's phone rang, he didn't know who or what to expect. It was part of what kept life interesting. On that July day, it was Charlie Roxbury calling, the adjunct responsible for all of Great Britain.

"Ned, Charlie here," the American said, with a tinge of British creeping in—Charlie had been posted to London for over three years.

"What can I do you for, stranger?"

"I'm set for a two-week holiday. My first break since that Chunnel bombing. One of these Nordic cruises. All paid up in full. In advance, you see. Can't get a nickel back if I don't go on the damn thing."

"What's the problem, Charlie?" As Ned said this man's name, Vicky looked over, eavesdropping. Vicky knew everybody's business.

"Wondering if you could take the helm for a fortnight, old friend. Goose the Lizzy for me." Lizzy Wainwright, Roxbury's name for his vintage Jaguar coupe. Charlie was well aware of Ned's love of a fast car. The offer of the loan of the cherished car made Ned suddenly cautious.

"Adjunct to London?" Gorman inquired. "You're joking, right?"

"It's all been cleared with the brass. All you need to do is say yes."

"Yes!" Gorman crowed.

"You may want to know that it's not all fun and games. Word on the street here is that military plastics have gone missing. Semtex. We're verifying as we speak, but if true, you have your work cut out for you. The case would be yours."

"Until you got back."

"The case is yours, Neddie, not mine. You would stay on indefinitely. Until we recover or account for the missing explosives."

"Indefinitely? You're answering my dreams here."

"It might run the two weeks. It might run a month or more. Dog work, I'm afraid. Serious shit, missing explosives. But I'd play Watson once I'm back."

"How long have you had these tickets, Charlie?" Ned Gorman smelled a rat. It seemed entirely possible that the cruise had been arranged after word of the missing explosives had reached Roxbury's desk. Any such investigation would remain open until cleared, and if the explosives were to do any damage in the meantime, the Special Agent in charge of the investigation would bear the brunt of the responsibility. Gorman saw this coming, but the lure of a foreign desk remained a strong temptation.

"I've had this planned for months, Ned. I'm not dumping a black hole on you."

"How do I know that?"

"Ned, it's me."

"Nashville is still quite present in my mind, Charlie, old boy. Why don't you fax me some proof you've had these tickets for several months. Okay? I get that fax, and you're on board ship."

"On its way to you," Roxbury said. Had he been expecting this request?

"Your flat in Hampstead?" Gorman requested.

"Of course."

"And Lizzy."

"She's all yours."

"Why does this sound too good to be true?" Ned Gorman asked.

"Because she is. Her name is Melanie, my friend. The passage is for two. Premier cabin. Eleven days at sea with a twenty-four-year-old with legs to the ceiling and insatiable appetites. She's MI5, so we can even speak the same language. Would you pass up that opportunity?"

"To whom do I speak on this end?" Gorman asked.

"The Vulture has the papers. She signed off on it, Neddie. It's all yours, I'm telling you."

The pooled fax machine hummed with an arrival. Gorman knew it was from Roxbury. The guy never wasted a minute. "Have a nice cruise."

"Double-clutch when you're downshifting."

"Of course."

"And Neddie . . . Maybe I'll see you when I get back."

Gorman hung up the phone, but again his stomach churned. In his job nothing was ever as it seemed. Part of the fun. Part of the problem.

Billy Sprague offered his blue blazer to the flight attendant in Virgin Atlantic's Upper Class cabin, hesitating a moment to allow the woman sitting in the aisle seat to realize he needed to get past her. The woman was a blonde. Shoulder length. Sun bleached. She wore a set of stereo headphones provided by the carrier, nodding her head to a loud beat that trailed out the plastic ear cups. A tomato cocktail—a Bloody Mary?—sat half empty on the center armrest that separated the seats. As the blonde finally looked up, Sprague recognized her as Rita Shaughnessy, from the ladies' tour. She spent more time in the supermarket tabloids than she did on the tour, more of a celebrity than a golfer, but at one time the longest driver to wear a skirt. Excluding the Scottish men, he realized, trying to adapt to the culture of his destination.

"Window seat," Sprague said.

"What are you drinking?" Rita asked.

"Beer," Sprague told the flight attendant, who immediately began to prattle on about the various brews on board. "Bud," he said, cutting her short.

Rita slipped off the headphones and scooted up in the seat, not sitting but not standing, forcing Sprague to slip past her and making sure he experienced her anatomically as he did. Sprague excused himself with the contact. Rita told him, "No problem." The guy was tan, tall, and his eyebrows were nearly white. She could have taken a bite of him if he'd offered. Maybe she'd encourage a membership in the Mile High Club before the flight was over,

depending on how the Valium mixed with the Bloody
Marys. Too much Valium and she couldn't get herself in
the mood for anything but TV. Upper Class offered each
passenger his or her own small TV with an enormous
selection of free movies. If need be, she'd just slug out for
the flight and take in the free flicks.

"Dos Lagos Open," Sprague said. "Four years ago. You
reached the green in one on eighteen. I've never seen anything like it. Not before. Not since."

"What a charmer!" Rita said, hoisting her drink. Not
waiting for his to arrive, she took a long pull. A double, it
burned just right going down. She added, "Four years is a
long time."

"Billy Sprague," he said, offering her his hand.

She juggled the drink and they shook hands. She let
hers be just a little limp, loving the firmness with which
he took it. The way she gripped a club she could have
squeezed the stainless out of stainless steel, and they both
knew it. "Do you play?" She hated hearing the golf stories.
It was all anyone ever talked to her about. There could
have been an earthquake an hour earlier, and yet it would
never be mentioned. Only the dogleg third and that awful
sand trap.

His beer was delivered. A partially empty can and a tall
beer glass bearing the airline's logo.

"If we get into that," Sprague said, "it'll be a busman's
holiday for both of us."

"You play professionally then," she said, not knowing
why she continued something she had no desire to discuss.

"Not in your league. A club pro is all. My afternoons
are middle-aged housewives who will never drive more
than a hundred and twenty and always three-putt. They'd

rather have me help them with their grip than their game, if you follow me."

"Oh, I'd follow you, all right. Wherever you led. Count on it." She drained the glass and hoisted it over her head, from where it was immediately whisked away by one of the half dozen flight attendants in the cabin.

Sprague said, "Did that lady say something about a free massage? Did I get that right?"

"They provide sleeping attire—gray sweats that you get to keep—a five-course dinner, free movies, a manicure or a neck and foot massage, champagne, an amazing selection of wines, and that little flight kit there in your pouch."

"But massage? Really?"

"I've flown Upper Class once before, and I'm telling you, it's better than most of the private jets I've been on." Her drink was returned, as if on cue.

"Isn't that Zamora over there?" Sprague whispered. "The window seat?"

"And the aisle is his caddy. Can you believe that shit? A fucking caddy in Upper Class. There ought to be rules or something."

"The Phillip Bates tournament?" Sprague asked.

She gave him a look. "You too?"

Sprague shrugged. "I'm as surprised as you are."

She thought for a moment. "There was a Bill Sprague who won the National Amateur one year, wasn't there? . . ."

"That was a while ago," he said.

"You never tried the Tour?" She was truly puzzled now.

"It's a long story."

"So now you hustle fat cats at some posh little club."

"Something like that," he said.

She shrugged. "You don't want to talk about it, it's okay with me." She raised her drink to him. "We all have our skeletons."

He lifted his beer in return. "Here's to Phillip Bates."

She nodded. "Do you know anything about this tournament?"

"Nothing whatsoever. Just the invite and the check and what I've seen on ESPN."

"Same here," she said. " 'Golf legends,' they call us. Makes me feel like I'm on the Senior tour."

Sprague glanced at her. "I wouldn't make that mistake."

She lifted an eyebrow. "So what do you think is up with the 'dozens of surprise guests'?"

"I wondered the same thing. That invite-list scrolls, and I was hard-pressed to think of one person who might have been left out."

"The ad kind of looked like one of those oldies-goldies collections. You know those ads?"

"I hate those ads," he said.

She laughed. "Yeah, me too."

She glanced over at him then, and they met eyes for the first time that mattered. This was no "hi, how ya doing?" meeting of the minds, but more like a zipless fuck that she felt clear down inside her, like he'd slipped his hand under her bottom when she wasn't looking. She said, "Well, as far as I'm concerned, this little outing is looking better by the minute. At least," she fished for a compliment, "it looks that way to me."

"Definitely," Sprague answered. He lowered his voice, leaned over the substantial armrest, and said, "Your agent say anything about 'saving the world'?"

"Honey," she said, laying a hand on his forearm and squeezing just right, "my agent is far more worried about me saving my own ass. The world'll have to wait."

London shone like a jewel despite the thick carpet of fog that hung suspended only a few yards above the city's skyline. Ned Gorman sat in the left-hand seat of a Ford sedan, his driver casually passing cars like they were standing still. The driving on the left instilled total terror in Ned, who kept leaning the wrong way with each pass.

"The situation is this," his British counterpart informed him. "We suspect the involvement of one François Le Tour, an environmental activist who we believe responsible for at least three animal-rights bombings and a ship arson that took out a container ship. He's Belgian. Single. Twenty-three. No current photographs."

"Suspect how?" Gorman asked. No time to enjoy the surroundings. So typical of the job to thrust him into the stolen explosives case before he'd even had a chance to shave. His head felt dull from fatigue. It was seven in the morning going on . . . he couldn't compute the time change, but it felt like the middle of the night.

"Obviously, we don't have an eyewitness," the driver joked, but Gorman wasn't in the mood.

"A snitch. Someone undercover. You can't tell me yet because it's Need To Know. My feelings aren't hurt, don't worry. It's just I have a bit of a headache, and I was hoping to put my feet up for a few hours."

"Not today, I'm afraid. Besides, it's better to push through the first day. Drink some tea. Make it through to dinner. It resets the clock much more quickly."

Gorman leaned the wrong way again, expecting to pass on the left. The car leaned right and the driver raced past.

"How much plastique?" Gorman asked.

"That is the bad news, I'm afraid. Upwards of twenty kilos."

"*Kilos!*" Gorman exclaimed. A quarter pound of Semtex could drop an average house. "Fifty *pounds* of Semtex?"

"You can understand our concern. He could take out the House of Lords, any of the bridges, Westminster Abbey."

"Fifty *pounds!*"

"Still feel like a nap?" the driver asked.

"How long has he had it?"

"Four days, if we're right."

"Le Tour stole it?"

"No. A bloke inside our own navy. We've identified him—he's being carefully watched and evaluated before we question him. Our information," the man said carefully, "is that Le Tour was the buyer."

"Four days is an eternity." Gorman thought this through. "But why involve us?" he asked. "Other than for a consult?" His dull mind churned through various possibilities. "The embassy? Is that it? You think he'll hit an American target? A corporation?"

"A golf tournament," the driver answered.

"A what?"

"Our informant promises us that Le Tour will be

heading to Edinburgh by rail today. The first afternoon train."

"Reliable?"

"We would like to think so." He added, "But of course we have no idea what he might look like. Only that twenty kilos won't make for light packing."

"A golf tournament? What's *that* got to do with the embassy adjunct?"

"It's one of yours, I'm afraid. Not ours."

"A U.S. golf tournament in Scotland? You've lost me."

"Phillip Bates," the driver said, delivering the car into a grave silence.

"*The* Phillip Bates?"

"You're not a golfer."

"Tree climber." When the driver looked over at him indifferently, Gorman added, "It's a long story."

"Phillip Bates purchased a very old Scottish castle and its grounds. Huge controversy," he said, pronouncing it with the emphasis on the second syllable so that Gorman was still trying to piece the word together as the man continued. "An enormous estate. Converted the countryside into an eighteen-hole course that may give St. Andrews a run for its money, if I hear right. He's throwing a bit of a do to inaugurate the thing. I'm amazed you haven't heard about it, quite frankly. He's launching the next generation of his operating system simultaneously. It's a weeklong affair. International television coverage. Quite a stage, frankly. We're involved because of the dignitaries, many of whom are traveling through London, one direction or the other."

"Dignitaries?"

"Bates has kept it close to his vest. If our intelligence is right, he's invited every damn political leader in the world to this tournament." He added, "And most appear to have accepted."

"And you make Bates and his tournament the target?"

"Our people do, yes."

"This is what I've inherited on my first day in London?" He moaned. "Charlie . . ."

"Bates cut down well over four hundred acres of Scottish old-growth forest, installed six new lakes, and seeded the entire course with genetically altered grasses. How's that for an environmental target?"

"Oh . . . my . . . God," Gorman uttered, his feet and fingers ice cold.

"Yes. Our sentiments exactly."

The car left the motorway traffic, taking a left-hand exit rather than following the stream of rubber and steel toward London proper. "Isn't the city that way?" Gorman inquired.

"City?" the driver replied. "Didn't I tell you? You're being choppered up the rail line to Oxford. The train leaves from there traveling directly to Edinburgh in"—he checked his watch—"thirty-six minutes. You'll be on that train, along with two of our own operatives."

"I will?"

"Oh yes, you most certainly will. And if we are lucky, Le Tour will be on that train as well."

Alfonzo Zamora showed his substantial girth dressed in the Upper Class gray sweats that served as pajamas for the flight. He hovered over Rita's aisle seat, apparently in need of a drool bucket.

"The Bates thing?"

"Yeah. Both of us," Rita answered, pointing to Sprague, who introduced himself and reached out a hand.

Zamora ignored Sprague and the man's extended hand, his interest solely in Rita's bustline. "Been reading stories about you, sweetheart."

"Down, Alfonzo," she said, helping Billy's extended arm away from her chest and then reaching for the drink, her own hand trembling slightly.

"Maybe we draw the same foursome. Play best ball. I heard firsthand the fucking president of Mexico is going to play. Maybe Fidel, even. Did you know he's a fucking four handicap?"

"So's Michael," Rita said. "M.J.," she supplied. "And that's firsthand knowledge too, Alfonzo."

"If the pope was ten years younger, he'd be shanking 'em with the rest of the in-crowd," Zamora roared, a little too loudly for the cabin. Zamora had been sampling the free champagne a little too liberally. "Fucking pope loves the politicians."

"Politicians?" Sprague asked, thinking back to the ominous words of his dead mentor. "As in world leaders?"

"Fidel, as in what, Schwartz? Is he your caddy or what?" Zamora asked her.

"If I were traveling with *my* caddy, Alfonzo, he wouldn't be sitting in Upper Class with me, now would he? Billy here took the Olympic gold medal in Atlanta."

"Bet that looks terrific on your mother's mantel," Zamora cracked sarcastically.

"Why *do* you travel with Hector so close by your side anyway?" She covered her mouth to conceal a contrived smile. "Don't tell me the stories about you two are true? Seriously, Alfonzo?"

"What stories?"

"Never mind."

"What stories?" Zamora persisted.

"Castro?" Sprague finally managed to articulate. "Fidel Castro is going to be at this event?"

"You gotta be a caddy."

"And the president of Mexico," Sprague connected. The third beer had bent him sideways.

"For real?" Rita asked the man standing to her side.

"On good authority," Zamora claimed. "Just like I heard you been through more clinics than back nines lately."

"I'm still driving two-fifty straight as your pecker."

"You ought to know," he said, his nose lifting as he sensed the arrival of dinner. He crossed the cabin without a goodbye, which meant to Rita Shaughnessy that he would be back.

"Known him for long?" Sprague asked her.

"I knew Alfonzo a little too well for a very short amount of time," she confessed. "An IBM thing in Scotts-dale. Ever since, he thinks he has first right of refusal or something. Ownership. You know the way the fucking Hispanics are with women." She reconsidered. "Well, maybe not, but you get the idea."

"You and him?"

"Me and *everyone* for a while there, if you believe the

51

Star. I could play it differently, but you'll hear that about me. What you believe, that's up to you. People just *love* to talk about me." She added, "Unfortunately, Alfonzo was for real. Caught me at a particularly weak moment. Percodan and Chivas Regal. That was a bad combo for me." She waved a bejeweled wrist in the air, making clanking sounds. "Some people can handle it. Not me. Ended up dropping the Chivas in favor of Stoli. Now *there* was a kick in the seat!" She asked, "Ever seen *Caddyshack*?"

"Sure."

"Chevy Chase's opening line about doing drugs? When he encourages his caddy to take drugs daily? I *love* that line! Now *that's* a cinemagraphic moment if there ever was one. Clark Gable, eat your heart out. 'Frankly, my dear, I don't give a damn!' I mean, get outta town! What's the big deal? *Serpico*—now there's a picture with some language in it!" Off she went, naming film after film, sometime during which their dinners were delivered. She ordered red wine with the fish, and vanished into her headphones.

Billy Sprague felt bedeviled by Doc Toland's final words. *You're going over there to save the world as we know it.* What had Doc known about the event? About Castro and the others? About Billy's role in the tournament? Save the world? Billy thought. He felt as if he deserved to be no more than a caddy, just as Zamora had suggested. Alfonzo Zamora. Rita Shaughnessy. He didn't dare look around. There were probably other legends on board as well. To caddy would be a privilege in such company. And the money! All that, plus expenses and travel for a week of golf in Scotland? But saving *the world as we know it* . . . that pushed at his temples, robbed his appetite. He stared at the mango chutney fish course on his plate, unable to eat. He owed Doc. He'd do anything for Doc. Anything! But save the world? How the fuck did a person do that?

Gorman met a man named Thomas Franklin and a woman, Edna Zuckerman, on the footbridge at Oxford station that spanned the two sides of the platform, tracks running north and south. Passengers lugging suitcases and duffel bags walked past them in both directions.

Zuckerman, a dark-eyed, athletic-looking type in her late twenties, had lit a cigarette, annulling Gorman's first impression. She had wide hips and thick calves and a curiously tranquil face that he might have expected more from a nun. She wore a black leather jacket and a knee-length gray skirt with black tights. He would have thought slacks for a job like this, but maybe that was why she had worn the skirt. Gorman had found members of the intelligence community, as a group, to be the most fickle, the most unpredictable, the most quirky he'd ever met. He had to put himself into that camp, of course, what with a love of model trains, fast cars, and California wines. But the international set never ceased to amaze him.

Thomas Franklin, at thirty, looked more fortysomething, with his bald spot and bad teeth. His green tie held some hollandaise, his right French cuff some mustard or yellowing toothpaste. His right eye hung slightly lower on his face than his left, as if he'd been crushed in the birth canal. He spoke in a gravelly voice with a thick Gaelic accent, making him nearly impossible to understand.

"Three minutes," Franklin said. He handed both of the others a small device the size of a Palm Pilot. "It's called an E-nine," he said, "for Electric Canine. Electronic sniffer," he explained. "Has to come within twelve to twenty inches of the explosive to sense it. I've turned off the audible alert because we don't want these things chirping and alerting our boy we're on to him. But a red light illuminates if it smells trouble, so what we do is walk a car and check the lights on the sniffer. If we've got a red light then we know our boy is somewhere in that particular car, and we can try to narrow it from there. Okay?"

"Three minutes? I should have stopped at the loo," Zuckerman complained, glancing down the tracks. She told Gorman, "Whenever I get nervous I have to pee."

"Makes her hell in bed," Franklin growled.

"Don't you just wish," she snapped back at him. She turned to Gorman and glowed, suddenly a girlish child. "Do you like the States?"

"Shouldn't we get down to the platform?" Gorman encouraged.

"We'll meet in the dining car every half hour on the quarter hour," Franklin instructed, assuming control. Gorman stiffened. His impression was that it was to be his operation, that these two were his backup.

"If that's the way our friend wants it," Edna Zuckerman said, correctly reading Gorman's thoughts.

Gorman jumped in. "The dining car is fine. We don't

make contact unless there's something to share." He checked his watch. Remaining up inside the covered bridge instead of making for the platform made him nervous.

All three continually scanned the passengers below, making short comments like, "How about the bloke by the trash bin?" "The couple by the little kid there . . . That looks like a heavy valise." "The conductor doesn't look like he knows what he's doing." And each would then observe and inspect the individual in question, making a mental note so that they might be identified later.

"You and I will travel as a couple," Gorman instructed Zuckerman, who seemed delighted with this arrangement. "I'm visiting for the first time, and you're pointing out everything we're going to do and how much fun we're going to have." To Franklin he said, "You'll hit on her a couple of times when we're all in the dining car. Especially if there's information to pass. Or you'll flirt with him," he told Zuckerman. "Either way. Just make it convincing. I'll complain, and the other of you will either deny the flirting or claim to be old friends. Something that allows us to engage."

"The old friends thing is better," Franklin said, not taking his eyes off the various passengers. "What about that long-haired bloke, with the cane? He'd be about the right age, wouldn't he?"

Zuckerman agreed. "Good eyes, Tommy. Yes. Brilliant! The cane is meant as a disguise to throw us off the scent."

Gorman reminded, "We should keep in mind that we're looking for burns to the hands, or a man who never removes his gloves. Our experience is that these bombers inevitably have screwed up once or twice and carry trophies on their arms and hands."

"Brilliant!" Edna Zuckerman said again. "And you and me, Mr. Gorman? How friendly is this to be then? Lovers? School chums? How do we play it?"

"She wants to drop her knickers for you in the loo," said a jealous Franklin.

"Bugger off!" Zuckerman objected, smacking her comrade in the shoulder and knocking him off balance.

Gorman said softly, "In case we've been noticed up here, I would suggest we play the old friend angle in the dining car." He had one person in mind as he said this, an old, haggard-looking fellow perched on a bench below who seemed to be studying faces as much as they all were. "Any other agents on the train?" he asked. "I'm thinking about that old guy on the bench."

Individually, and quite professionally, Franklin and Zuckerman took turns observing the man in question.

"Got him," Franklin said.

"Likewise," Zuckerman echoed.

"That makes six or seven prime candidates."

"Plus another couple of hundred folks to pick from once everyone boards the train," Franklin reminded.

"School chums?" Edna Zuckerman inquired, glancing into her purse as if attempting to decide which lipstick to wear.

"Former lovers," Gorman informed her. "We're nervous around each other. Awkward—"

"Shouldn't be hard for Edna," Franklin interrupted. "Can't pour a cup of tea without spilling all over."

"Hush!" she fired back. To Gorman she said, "Former lovers it is, Ned. May I call you Ned?"

"Leave now," Gorman instructed Franklin. "You'll start at the front of the train and work your way back. We'll do the reverse."

"Assigned seats on the Edinburgh run, Yankee boy," Franklin corrected. "We'll look stupid if we don't head to our seats first. You two will have to get some bloke to switch seats if you're to sit together."

"That'll be my job," Zuckerman volunteered.

"With that blouse you're wearing, all you'll have to do is bend over to win yourself a favor." Franklin said to Gorman, "She's stacked, though you'd never know it with the blood-constricting bras she wears."

"You've always wanted to put your face in them," Edna Zuckerman countered. "And you'll never get your chance, Tommy boy. Not with that attitude of yours." She sounded a little Irish. By this point Gorman was catching about every other word of their dialogue.

The train arrived from behind them.

Gorman reminded, "Twenty kilos, don't forget. Enough to leave a crater a quarter mile wide and a hundred feet deep."

Franklin turned and said softly, "Bates wanted to launch this new software with a bang. If we cock this up, maybe he gets the chance."

The train to Edinburgh rode smoothly, given its incredible speed. Nothing like Amtrak, Gorman realized, wondering how the United States could fall so behind in a given technology when it prided itself on maintaining the leading edge. The rolling green hills streamed past like a living oil painting. Rock walls. Stone churches. Clusters of blond-rock Cotswolds villages in the distance in breathtaking panoramas that held his face glued to the quiet glass window instead of searching the car for would-be bombers.

Edna Zuckerman negotiated the seat exchange with a single eyelid-fluttering request, so that now she and Gorman sat side by side, her black tights exposed and inviting, her leather jacket folded on the floor, her white blouse vaguely translucent.

Gorman made a quick seat count and estimated that they had upward of four or five hundred passengers riding the train's ten cars, one of whom might be carrying enough plastique to level Madison Square Garden. His scalp itched. His stomach ached from too much coffee and not enough sleep. He'd lost track of how many hours he'd been awake. He nodded off watching the scenery, coming awake to a mirror image of himself kissing the glass and drooling down its surface. Zuckerman's seat was empty. He caught a brief glimpse of her as she slipped out of the electronically controlled car doors, heading up the train. He checked his watch. Twenty minutes had been stolen from him. He stood and headed toward the back of the car, determined to find Le Tour and devise a way to get him off the train and away from that plastique.

Would he know by a look? he wondered as he slowly moved from seat to seat, using each to balance himself even though it wasn't necessary—the train ran so comfortably it proved difficult to tell it was moving. Gorman made a point of stealing a look at each and every passenger, though never deliberately nor heavy-handedly. A woman and her daughter. A grammy with her knitting. Businessmen. Businesswomen. Tourists. Tourists. More tourists. He heard more American accents than British. Backpacks. Briefcases. Duffels. Roller cases. Aluminum. Rip-stop nylon. Leather. Suddenly the task before him seemed insurmountable.

He stopped at the end of the car and ducked into the coffin-size restroom. The E-9 showed no red lights. He slipped it back into his pocket, knowing he had to come up with a way to get it closer to the overhead racks where most of the luggage was kept. There were also luggage bins at both ends of the cars, but Le Tour wasn't likely to leave his explosives so available. In fact, it seemed more likely the man would keep it under the seat in front of him, now that Gorman thought about it. And that could narrow the field considerably, given that most people wanted the extra legroom.

Gorman's head was beginning to feel leaden. He stopped thinking for a moment, urinated, and washed his face, then studied his weathered look in the mirror, wondering why he had accepted Roxbury's offer. Explosives. The world's most successful and wealthiest entrepreneur. A global party. Golf! He wasn't simply over his head, he was on the bottom of the Marianas Trench looking up.

The next car and the next, no red light. A half dozen or so briefcases kept on the floor under the seat—more than Gorman would have guessed. Laptop computers, he imagined, wondering if twenty kilos of plastique could fit inside such a small case. Then it occurred to him for the first time that Le Tour did not need more than a pound or two of his stash to wreak considerable damage and loss of life, and this thought depressed him, because Le Tour would also think to hermetically seal the explosive in multiple layers of heavy-mil plastic, to wipe the outside of each layer with pure alcohol before sealing the next. Le Tour might use couriers, might even slip the explosives—however disguised—into someone else's luggage, perhaps even doing so at the luggage compartments at either end of the train cars, the very compartments Gorman had ruled out as too public. These thoughts swirled inside his head, dizzying and fatiguing.

The possibility of a courier increased his suspect population to now include women, whom he had all but ruled out previously. He reached the end of the train—a locked luggage car—turned around, and started through the cars once again, every face a potential killer, every case a potential bomb. Twenty minutes later he stepped through an electronic door into the dining car. A woman grabbed him from behind, spun him around, and kissed him on the lips.

"I thought you'd ditched me!" Edna Zuckerman complained when she pulled away from the kiss.

A stunned and overtired Gorman just stared into two eyes buried in mascara. He wiped off lipstick from his lips. "Exercise," he said, recovering. "Been walking off that breakfast."

"Tea?"

"Why not?"

"Come on." She grabbed his hand and pulled him through the car like a child eager to show a parent a new toy. She turned and kissed him again. "No red light," she whispered into his ear.

He held her close. "Same here," he said.

"What next?"

"I'm thinking courier," he told her.

She laughed loudly enough for everyone to take notice of her. She reminded him all at once of Bette Midler. "Here?" she gasped as if Gorman had propositioned her.

"Tea," he said.

"There you are!" came a male voice.

Gorman looked up to see Franklin coming toward them.

"Thought I'd lost you!" Franklin said.

Gorman pulled Edna close to him possessively, the curtain up on act one of *Edna Does Neddy*, the roles defined. Only the script remained to be provided. He and Franklin shook hands as Zuckerman introduced them. They leaned in together, all three faking laughs. Franklin said, "Zero."

"No hits," Gorman confirmed in a practiced voice that did not carry. He turned to the bar to order two teas, leaving his girlfriend and the stranger to share a private conversation, all the while glancing over at them as if convincingly concerned he might loose Edna to the interloper.

All in a day's work. Ned Gorman's body begged for a few hours' sleep.

With his mind dulled by time zones and his body jazzed by tea, Gorman arrived at a solution to the problem of so much overhead luggage avoiding his electronic sniffer.

Solutions to problems were often so simple *"if you allow them to be"*—as he had once been taught by an academy spook. All he did was place the E-9 in an outer flap of one of his own suitcases and then attempt to find a home for the suitcase. The process involved playing a jet-lagged American, too stupid to boil water, moving from car to car as he tried to create a space in the overhead luggage racks. This brought his suitcase in physical contact with dozens of others and, in proximity to the rest, allowed him to steal a look at his sniffer between cars in hopes of confirming the existence of the plastique.

When overly tired, Ned Gorman's ears tended to ring and his head felt heavy, as if filled to overflowing with congealed Jell-O. He worked a couple seconds behind real time, as if some kind of electronic delay had been installed in his brain. He lost hold of thoughts as quickly as he formed them, condemned then to mine his subconscious and retrieve them to the surface. Like speaking in an echo chamber.

This helped explain why, at the rear of car seven, as he stooped to lift the suitcase flap and check the electronic sniffer, he suddenly wondered if he had forgotten to check the device one car earlier. He couldn't remember much of anything, except that he'd certainly checked this damn thing enough times over the last half hour, and if he'd left out one car, what the hell?

A red light blinked on the device.

Gorman stared at it and nearly resealed the luggage flap before connecting the thought and verifying that the sniffer had detected explosives. As his heart began to feel like a bass drum in a Main Street parade, Gorman reminded himself that "false-positives" were not uncommon in these less sophisticated portable sniffers. It doesn't necessarily mean explosives, he reminded himself. But of course the greater part of him was screaming: EXPLOSIVES!

He reset the device, staying on the floor and kneeling over his suitcase long enough to block traffic, so that when the door hissed open and he found himself staring into the crotch of a pair of blue jeans, and those jeans turned out to be occupied by a very attractive woman, he muttered an apology as that crotch, pressured from behind, rubbed the back of his head as he ducked out of the way and the passengers squeezed past, the woman basically straddling his head to get past him.

It wasn't a false-positive. He knew this intuitively, since his job on board this train was to locate explosives and the person carrying them. He glanced up, past the woman's blue jeans, to see the back of a man carrying a suitcase heading for the far end of the car. His eyes jumped to the overhead rack where, midcar, he spotted a hole in the crowded luggage rack that had not been there a minute earlier. This time his numb brain reacted before his body, and he stumbled as he leapt to his feet, falling forward over his own bag and pulling down Miss Blue Jeans with him as he went. There was some chortling in the seats, and a few strong arms quickly came to the assistance of the downed woman, while Gorman was left to fend for himself. He apologized to the woman, and though determined to now pass her, waited for her to collect herself and brush herself off and lead the way down the narrow aisle. The stainless steel door at the far end of the car hissed shut. Gorman lost sight of his suspect.

"I lost him," he explained to Edna Zuckerman. They stood together in the cramped bathroom of car five, adjacent to the dining car. She smeared some lipstick on his lips and cheek, loosened his tie, and rebuttoned his shirt incorrectly as they talked. Should anyone encounter two people leaving a bathroom together, she wanted it to look as if they'd had sex. She dabbed some water onto her face, checking the mirror to make sure it looked like perspiration.

"We don't know it was him."

"No," he agreed. "And I couldn't very well go trying my little ruse all over again, stuffing my suitcase up there like that."

"So he could still be wherever he was in the first place—if that wasn't him you saw leaving the car."

"I was in car seven. Quite honestly, I'm not convinced I checked the E-nine after car six. I'm a little jet-lagged. It could be either." He added, "And if it was him I saw leaving car seven, then he could be anywhere at this point."

"The bag?"

"Black nylon."

"Terrific."

"I know," he agreed. One of hundreds on the train.

"But he's on here," she said.

"*Could* be on here," he corrected.

"I'd say it's damn likely he's on this train," she said.

"Or a courier," he reminded. "Knowingly or unknowingly."

"And the one with the bag?" she asked.

"May have wanted to brush his teeth or change a shirt or not leave his cash behind when he went to buy a sandwich."

"But he didn't go to buy a sandwich. You lost him. Lost sight of him," she corrected herself, attempting to lay less blame on Gorman. "Listen," she suggested, "I can place the sniffer in my handbag and check cars six and seven a second time. Go from piece to piece of luggage as if I've lost my own."

"That would work." He mumbled, "Golf clubs."

"What?"

"Have you noticed all the bags of golf clubs?"

"Time of year," she agreed.

"And each with a dozen zippers. If I'm our boy, and I'm looking for a blind courier—someone who has no idea he or she is being used—I slip the plastique into a golf bag. And you know why? Because no one is going to touch their clubs until they're out on a course. It's a perfectly safe place to hide something for the duration of the train trip."

She nodded excitedly. "I like that!"

The train rocked uncharacteristically, and she fell into him in full frontal contact so that they hugged like long-lost friends. Her hand unexpectedly cupped his crotch. As she stood back up, regaining her balance, he saw red in her cheeks, and that struck him as cute. He felt seventeen again.

"Balls," she said, letting go of him down there.

His turn to blush. "Excuse me?"

"Golf balls. What if Le Tour had the plastique made

into golf balls? Could be done overnight, I would think. He then hides the balls in some stranger's bag. If he doesn't get the balls out before the end of the train ride, he follows that bag to whatever hotel it's headed toward and pinches it there."

Gorman pointed out, "We're standing in a bathroom talking about pinching balls."

She grinned and lowered her voice. "At least it will sound right if anyone's attempting to eavesdrop." She unbuttoned her blouse one too many buttons, reached in and tugged her breast and bra so that she nearly spilled out. "You ready?" she asked. He was ready. If she felt him now she would know that. But he didn't answer her. "Wait in the dining car," she instructed. "Find Franklin and catch him up on the latest. I'll sweep six and seven a second time and report back to you."

"Got it," he said.

"Wait . . . You don't look authentic enough." She pulled herself to him and laid a kiss on his lips that briefly stopped his heart. She smeared her lips on his and pressed closely enough to feel through his trousers that he wasn't ignoring her. She leaned back and studied him. In a warm and creamy voice she said, "Brilliant! I believe this assignment is starting to grow on me." She unlocked the door and said privately, "Growing on you too, I see."

"Are you staying in London or heading straight up to Scotland?" Billy Sprague asked Rita Shaughnessy as the flight attendant delivered the four-cheese omelets, pain au chocolat, grapefruit, and mimosas.

"Is that a come-on?" Shaughnessy inquired.

"I don't think so," Sprague answered, "but I'm drunk enough it just might be."

"The Brown," she said.

Sprague looked at his plate, believing this comment of hers had something to do with the food. A lot of yellows, but only the chocolate was brown. He took a bite of the pastry. "Delicious," he said.

"I'm staying at the Brown for two nights," she said. "Adjust to the time change, shop for some evening wear—I hear Bates has some monumental parties planned—and get as high as possible. If I'm hearing right, maybe I can add getting laid to that list."

He sprayed chocolate onto the back of the seat in front of him, wiped up, and tried to pretend she hadn't said that. "I'm at the Brown too."

"Bates," she said. "I bet fat-ass and his caddy are with us as well."

"He likes you," Sprague observed.

"Listen. Alfonzo pinned me to an elevator wall one night when my vision was poor. In Spanish, our little run-in apparently translates to some kind of ownership, like a stock option or something. Vaguely related to 'possession is nine-tenths,' I think. Never mind that all I heard was the accent and I thought I was in the elevator with Nicky Moran. The girls on the tour are always talking about Nicky's driver—if you catch my drift—and there I was with a chance to tee up. And I grabbed it—so to speak." She delivered all this while filling her mouth with both the four-cheese omelet and the mimosa, so that some of the words garbled. "What a disappointment!"

"You have a thing going with him?" he asked, slow on the uptake.

"Had," she clarified. "Just that once." She said deliberately, "And it was a very short, very uninteresting *thing*."

"So maybe we could grab a dinner together."

"We could grab a lot together," she suggested, attracted to his tan and physique. So many of the pros let their bodies go. Not this one. "But if it's dinner you want, I'd suggest the Ivy. The concierge can book it for us."

"I think he should."

"Eight? Eight-thirty?"

He checked his watch, which he had reset to London time, wondering if it could possibly be before noon. It felt like four in the morning. "Dinner's a long way away."

"We could try lunch in my suite," she suggested provocatively, "so long as I'm on Bond Street for my fitting by two-thirty."

Sprague took a stab at the omelet. He asked her, "Have you ever thought of a round of golf as a way to save the world as we know it?"

"Only when I'm dead broke." She added, "Which is pretty much all the time lately. Then it's sink or swim."

"I mean literally," he corrected.

"Save the world?" she asked, bemused.

"Yes."

"I can't think of anything less important to the world than a golf score. Can you?"

"Not really. No."

"Then why the question?"

"Zamora's mention of the politicians," Sprague answered, skewing the truth.

"You mean if Mubarak and Qaddafi are in the same foursome and Mubarak wins? Something like that?"

"Maybe so," he answered. "I'm not quite sure. That's why I asked the question in the first place."

"You're tired and you've been drinking. I wouldn't give it much consideration."

"Oh, but I do."

"I think we should focus on the present. The moment. Don't you? Like lunch in my suite. I'd like to unpack and take a bath first. We could say around . . . noon. What do you think?"

"Or maybe it's more a question of opportunity. If you're in a foursome with some Balkan dictator, do you play nice or do you pull out a knife and run him through?"

"Jesus, you're hung up on this. That's awful, what you just said. There's course etiquette, you know? You don't stab someone on a green. It just isn't done."

"And all those guys who get fried by lightning every year? What about them? Lifting their putter in anger and a bolt of lightning frying them on the spot. Is that a certain kind of justice? A similar justice to what I'm talking about?"

"If Qaddafi gets fried by lightning," she suggested, "there won't be a lot of tears shed. I'll give you that. But if a course pro from the Midwest runs a butter knife through his heart, there's a slightly different spin to it, don't you think?"

"I'm not so sure there is."

"Are you telling me I've got the hots for a psychopath?"

she asked disappointedly. "Just my luck: if they aren't gay, they're fucking crazy."

"No butter knives," he said. "It's the *concept* that interests me. The ethics. The responsibility to our fellow man. It's that old question: if you knew what you know now about Hitler, but you knew it back then, say four years before he came into power, and you met him in a bar, do you kill him on the spot or do you let him live?"

"I ask him to buy me a drink," she answered, accepting another mimosa from a sweating stainless steel pitcher poured by the flight attendant. "And I take it from there."

"But take it where?"

"You think too much," she complained, consuming half the mimosa in a single swig. "Can't we just keep this as lunch in my suite at twelve-thirty? How's *that* for a concept?"

"And the Ivy for dinner," he said.

"At least you're listening," she said. "That's a start."

Waiting for Edna Zuckerman to return from her sweep of the train cars, Ned Gorman spotted a man at the dining car bar, a black nylon suitcase at his feet. He couldn't be sure it was the same man he had seen leaving car seven in a hurry, but he couldn't say it wasn't that man either. All at once his depth of fatigue vanished, replaced by a speeding heart and prickling skin. Le Tour? A courier? An innocent passenger? He nudged past two American couples complaining about the exchange rate and England's refusal to support the Euro.

The man at the bar either sensed him or happened to look back, but either way he briefly met eyes with the approaching Gorman. Given his dark features and a serious tan, the brown-eyed man looked surprisingly nondescript to a federal agent trying to memorize his features. The tan could have been cosmetics, the hair a wig, the eye color contact lenses. Average height. Average age—early thirties perhaps.

The man lowered his plastic cup of tea, picked up his nylon bag, and calmly walked away from Gorman, who was blocked by a fat woman with a small child.

There was nothing abrupt about the man's actions—he moved smoothly and with control—and yet Gorman wanted to interpret them as those of a man attempting to escape.

The dining car was positioned in the middle of the Edinburgh train, five passenger cars to either side of it, a locomotive and baggage car to the front, a solo baggage car to the rear. Gorman heard the far door hiss, although his sight of it remained blocked by the curving bar. He nudged past the fat woman, dodged a man carrying a pair of beers, and ran smack into another group of Americans, this time discussing how expensive the train service was. By the time he reached the end of the car, triggering one door open and then the next, the man with the nylon bag had disappeared again.

He spun around. Through the two layers of thick glass he saw that the dining car ended with a public restroom. The suspect might have ducked into the restroom while intentionally tripping the door to open, hoping to confuse

Gorman. He glanced right, down the long empty aisle of the passenger car where he stood. Probably a restroom down there as well. He scanned the backs of heads, checking if the suspect had taken a seat. The man had been wearing a black leather jacket and blue jeans—he and a few hundred others, Gorman realized.

The door hissed behind him. He spun quickly around.

"Any luck?" Thomas Franklin asked softly, taking a moment to edge by him.

Gorman tried to push him out of the way in order to see past, his head swiveling from between this passenger car and the adjacent dining car. "Had him. Lost him," he said.

"Our boy?"

"A possible," Gorman answered. "Dark hair, average height, black nylon—"

"The same man you saw—"

"We picked up an E-nine positive in car six or seven. Edna's making another pass."

"Edna is it?"

"Zuckerman," Gorman corrected, still frantically looking one way then the other. "I'm brain dead. Too tired. Not thinking clearly."

"I'll take the forward cars," Franklin whispered. "Calm down. We're all right, you know. It's a train. He's not going anywhere."

"Could be a courier. Doesn't mean it's our boy."

"Calm down," Franklin repeated.

"That's him!" Gorman crowed.

The two men looked through the void of space that separated the two cars. The suspect was heading right for them.

"Him?" Franklin whined. "Are you kidding me? That's Fernando Gaspara. Won at Winged Foot in ninety-six. You do know *something* about golf, don't you?"

"A golf pro?" Gorman replied, disappointed. "But I thought . . . I know the game, not the players."

"You thought wrong. Let's find Zuckerman. We want those explosives in custody *before* we reach Edinburgh. If they make it off this train . . . Well, it's your ass, not mine."

Chapter Three

HUNG UP ON THE LIP

by Tami Hoag

Rathgarve Castle, Scotland

"I *hate* bloody golf!" Angus MacLout declared in a burr as thick as a Highland mutton stew.

He peered through the shrubbery at the course that rolled over some of the most beautiful countryside in all of Scotland. Rathgarve, the gray granite castle that stood on the crest of the hill, had occupied that ground for so many hundreds of years that it had taken on the look of something natural to the earth, as if it were but a strange outcropping or a cairn of the giants of Gaelic lore.

Great swaths had been cut through the ancient forest, making way for fairways. Hillocks had become flag-studded greens. Banks had become bunkers. Water hazards had been added, the largest one being christened "Nessie" by the blathering idiots from ESPN.

"Daft, boring game. I'd sooner watch people sleep."

"Aye, you always were a bit queer that way, Angus," Sheena Cameron said. "I recall you being sent to the pastor for a talking-to after you got caught watching your grandmother sleep in her brassiere and garters. Remember that, Ox?"

Sheena was as petite and pretty as Ox Ferguson was stout and ugly. Black hair cropped short and stylish. Eyes as big and blue as a Scottish loch. A face like a pixie with porcelain skin. She was dressed in black from head to toe: tight slacks, turtleneck, and black leather biker jacket. She had slipped past security at a weak spot—a guard overly susceptible to a wink and a grin and an empty promise of something more. Men were such fools. Most of them, anyway.

Unable to rely on such charms, Angus and Ox had come in the honest way: as employees assigned to groundskeeping duties.

Ox replied with the same grunt he used for all questions, whether his answer was intended to be affirmative or negative. His head was wreathed and swathed in red hair that obscured his every facial feature. It was the hair as much as his physique that had earned him his nickname. That and a tendency to drool when he'd had too much ale.

Angus sent Sheena a ferocious scowl. "How many times do I have to tell you? I feared her dead. It was all a great misunderstanding, is all."

"Uh-huh." Sheena dismissed the topic and snatched the binoculars away from him. Binoculars: a grand name for what Angus had brought. "Opera glasses," she grumbled. "What all the great criminal masterminds use."

"They serve the purpose now, don't they? And saved the hundred pounds or better you'd have had me spend."

"I can't see a bloody thing."

"Blinded by obstinateness, you are."

"And you'll be forever constrained by the limits of your stingy, tiny mind, Angus MacLout. Dried and shriveled it is. Like a prune, like a *raisin*—no, like a *currant*." She turned to Ox. "What's smaller than a currant?"

His expression never altered. "The seed of a currant."

"Siding with her now, are you?" Angus accused, eyes wild, his long, raw-boned face contorted with outrage.

Ox went back to the grunt.

"Siding with Miss World Traveler. Miss I've-Been-to-the-Continent. Miss I-Know-It-All," he went on, posing and posturing, sticking his butt out and arching his back, prancing around and rolling his eyes.

Sheena turned away and squinted through the opera glasses. The lawns of the great castle were swarming with an army of people, a commotion the likes of which the place hadn't seen since the uprising of 1745. Television people and tournament officials, caterers and groundskeepers and God knew who-all. Plenty of security agents, to be sure, she noted. They were conspicuous in dark sunglasses, talking into the sleeves of their golf sweaters. They represented a variety of nationalities and agencies from all over the globe. Staking out the territory. Sniffing out potential trouble spots around the castle and over the course.

Helicopters had swept over the grounds and the surrounding countryside for two solid days, scanning a perimeter of a mile in every direction. She'd gathered that bit of news from an RAF lad with too many hormones and too much beer on his brain. The helicopters would be up again as soon as the wind dropped.

Even as she thought it, a gust swept beneath one of the huge green-striped tents that had been staked out on the lawn, attempting to turn it into a giant balloon. Papers blew across the lawn like a flock of white birds, chased by half a dozen frantic people.

"I love the wind," she said, grinning. "Nature's full of chaos, she is. Chaos and temper. And vengeance."

Being from a long line of bitter, vindictive women, Sheena had a special warm spot in her heart for the notion of vengeance. It glowed red now as she let her gaze sweep over the acres, seeing devastation in the manicured beauty. Four hundred acres of ancient trees gone, replaced by grass cooked up in a laboratory by some mad scientist just waiting for his chance to clone a new race of humans. Evil. And Phillip Bates was the devil's right hand.

She looked at Angus over her shoulder. "You're still committed to this nonsense?"

"Aye. How many times do I have to tell you, woman?"

"You ought to *be* committed," she grumbled.

"And it's not nonsense!" he insisted, a little slow on the uptake. "I'm in the right and no one will hear me!" he ranted.

Sheena shushed him, frantically glancing around. "*Everyone* will hear you, you bloody great oaf! Lower your voice!"

"Two hundred years of injustice!" he raged on in a

hoarse whisper, spittle frothing at the corners of his mouth. "That land was not the MacGregors' to sell to Phillip Bates! It should have been *mine*! I am the last of the MacLouts, and the rightful heir to Rathgarve! The world will know it!"

He grabbed hold of her by the upper arms, hauling her up onto her toes, his white-rimmed eyes bugging out from under the wriggling brows. "Are you with me or agin' me, lass?"

"Don't be daft, man. I'm here, aren't I? As harebrained as this is, I'm with you, Angus. You know I have a soft spot for you," she cooed, batting her lashes. Then she made a little face. "It happens to be in my head."

"You're as good as a MacLout, girl!" he declared and kissed her full on the mouth, a wet, rubbery slobber of a kiss.

Sheena booted him one in the shin and wiggled away. "Don't insult the Camerons," she ordered, a wicked little smile playing at her lips. The light in her blue eyes danced. "I've got to go now. I'll call you tonight then, Angus. See if you can't keep Ox out of the phone box."

No one had ever seen Ox Ferguson use a telephone.

"Why you won't get a phone in your own house is beyond me," she muttered.

"Why pay all the time for a thing I use too little?" Angus said.

"Watch you don't ask him to buy you a pint, Ox," Sheena said, walking away. "He's liable to trade you in for a pet stone."

Ox grunted.

Rita Shaughnessy poked her head around the corner and looked both ways down the hall of the resplendent, clubby Brown's Hotel. Founded in 1837 by Lord Byron's valet, the place was like a grand country house smack in the heart of London. Wood paneling, grandfather clocks, antiques everywhere.

All was quiet on the fifth floor. The tourists had either taken themselves off for a full day of double-decker buses and taunting the guards at Buckingham Palace, or they had yet to rouse after a night of theater. Shushing herself, Rita rolled the rattling room service cart around the corner and down the hall, toward room 512. Anticipation and champagne bubbled in her bloodstream, and she resisted the urge to laugh out loud. Hot damn, this was fun.

Thank you, Phillip Bates, God of the Geek Boys. You know not what you do.

"And all the better that you don't, darling," she murmured.

She took a swig from one of two bottles in the silver ice bucket, dabbed delicately at her freshly painted lips with a linen napkin, and took a deep breath. She hadn't felt this good in God knew how long. And she wasn't even on anything. A paycheck, a tournament, and a guy all in one week. High on life.

"It's just great being me," she said under her breath, grinning.

Still, she wasn't content to just let things happen.

Seize the day. Sprague was liable to overthink her invitation and give himself an iceberg-size case of cold feet. Time for a full frontal Rita offensive.

She knocked at the door and stepped to the side. "Room service!"

There was a beat of silence. She stayed back against the door, out of peephole range.

"There must be some mistake. I haven't ordered anything."

"Compliments of Mr. Bates," she said, affecting a British accent that wasn't half bad.

"Oh. Oh . . . okay. Just a minute. I'm not dressed."

Rita felt herself light up like a slot machine hitting the jackpot. If her luck held this well through the weekend, she'd be acing every hole on the course. "That's perfectly all right, sir," she said. "If you would be so kind as to just open the door, I'll slip the tray in and leave you to your privacy."

Damn I'm good. She'd even remembered to pronounce it the way the Brits did: privacy with a short *i*. You might have thought the people who invented the damned language would have more respect for phonics.

The lock rattled in the door, and it opened an inch. Rita eased the cart back with her foot and pulled the door open, staying behind it.

"Thank you, sir. I'll have it in in a jiff."

Sprague disappeared into the suite, just a glimpse of a thick terrycloth robe and a pair of bare, hairy legs with the well-developed calves of a man who spent a lot of time walking up and down the hills of a golf course.

"And so will you, if I'm lucky."

Sprague wheeled around at the sultry change of voice,

knowing he probably looked like a cartoon character with his eyes bugging out and his jaw dropping to the floor. Rita Shaughnessy stood dead center in the sitting room of his suite, wearing a waiter's jacket, an apron, and a pair of stiletto heels. The smile that curled up the corners of her mouth was pure trouble, outdone only by the devilish light in her eyes.

She slipped the jacket back off her shoulders and dropped it.

"I believe you were going to have me for lunch, Mr. Sprague. And damned if it isn't high noon."

Alfonzo Zamora took the key out of his pants pocket and looked at the number engraved at the top. It was nothing but a blur. If it turned out that that bellman had slipped him the wrong key, he was going to find the guy and beat him to death with a nine-iron. For what he'd bribed the little Limey, he should have gotten Rita Shaughnessy naked on a silver platter.

Rita. Now there was something he didn't have *any* trouble seeing. Best piece of tail in golf spikes, and he didn't even mind so much that half the guys on the PGA Tour could vouch for the truth of the statement. He'd only had her once, and he'd had a marriage or two since, but he remembered that night with more clarity than a pint of tequila should have allowed. Hot, hot, habañero hot.

Zamora hitched up his pants and tried to smooth the

travel wrinkles out of his lucky yellow shirt. He hadn't taken time to shower after checking in, the need to find a bribable bellman a higher priority. But he had helped himself to the aftershave on the silver tray in the bathroom of the suite, slapping his face with it and rubbing a little under his arms. He sniffed the air now like a bull scenting for a cow, pleased with himself and his prospects.

Now, if he could just rekindle the flame with ol' Rita before she decided to have her way with the rube from East Buttcrack . . . How the hell had *that* guy gotten an invitation from Bates?

The door to 522 had been left slightly ajar. Could have saved himself three hundred bucks. Oh well. He pocketed the key. If things went well, he'd be needing it again.

Music was playing in the background as Zamora slipped into the room. Some kind of classical shit. Soothing—if you could stand it. The kind of music a woman might listen to while taking a bubble bath in the fancy tub of a swank hotel.

The fantasy spun itself fast-forward in his head: Rita up to her ears in bubbles; blond hair pinned up but messy; sticking one long, tanned leg up out of the foam to run a fat sponge along her shin; a bottle of champagne in a cooler at her elbow. That was enough to make his putter shudder.

But he could hear her rummaging around in the bedroom, and the fantasy bubble burst. Maybe later . . .

"Eh, *querida*," he called in his most sexy voice. "What do you say we play a little hole in one? I remember just how you like it."

She had her back to him as he entered the room.
Digging around in her suitcase. Or maybe it was her golf
bag. Either way, she was ass-end to him, which would
have been a fine view if his eyes hadn't been so fucked
up.

Then she came around, swinging something that connected with the side of his head like Tiger Woods
spanking a tee shot three hundred yards, and he didn't
see anything at all anymore.

"Well, let me tell you, honey," Rita said, collapsing back
against the mountain of feather pillows. "I don't know
about you saving the world, but you sure as hell rocked
mine. You been saving up or what?"

Sprague thought he might have blushed, if his circu-
latory system had still been capable of pushing blood to
his face. He lay flat on his back, one arm hanging off the
bed. He was pretty sure he was paralyzed. He'd never
thought of sex as an Olympic gymnastics event.

"Wow," was the only thing he could think to say.

Rita tilted over onto one elbow and looked down at
him. "That's the third wow you've given me, country
boy. Not that I don't appreciate it, but you're sounding
like a broken record."

"I think I may have had a stroke."

She chuckled wickedly, leaned down, and bit his
earlobe then traced the tip of her tongue around the
shell of his ear. "You've got a stroke all right. If you golf

like you fuck, honey, the PGA needs to clear the decks and make way for a star."

Memories of his brief, excruciating tour experience flashed across Sprague's mind like a dying comet. A cold fist tightened in the pit of his stomach. "I don't know what the hell I'm doing here."

"You seemed to know a few minutes ago."

"No. I mean at this tournament. Why would Phillip Bates invite *me*?"

"He admired you as an amateur. He had a vision about you. He drew your name out of a hat. What's the difference? You're here." She snuggled into him and nipped his shoulder. "And I'm here. *That's* the important thing."

Sprague paid her no mind, except to flinch when she bit. "I see Doc's hand in all of this. He's manipulating my life from beyond the grave."

"Doc? A people doc? Did he happen to leave you any 'script paper? Because I happen to know a pharmacist . . ."

"It's like a hero journey," Sprague said, staring at the ceiling. "Like in mythology. Like Obi-Wan Kenobi and Luke Skywalker in *Star Wars*."

"*Star Wars*." Rita sat up, pulling up the sheet with her to wipe the sweat from her brow. She raked her hair back out of her face and contemplated a shower as she glanced at the clock. "You know what was wrong with that movie? Luke was a wimp. Harrison Ford should have been the star of that movie. He can pilot my starship anytime he wants."

She could tell Sprague wasn't listening. He had apparently gone into some kind of catatonic trance where he was seeing himself singlehandedly taking on the forces of evil. Rita bent over and softly kissed his cheek. He was a sweet boy, even if he was one dot short of Yahtzee.

"Maybe ol' Doc forgot to tell you you're Superman," she said, slipping from the bed. "Time for me to go, Clark Kent. Cinderella has a date with the dressmaker."

"Nothing," Edna Zuckerman said on a stiff little sigh. She smiled for the benefit of the other travelers in the dining car, bent over with her hand on Gorman's shoulder, and kissed his cheek. "I went through cars six and seven both, and I've nothing to show for it but a pinched bottom. Can you believe the nerve of some people?"

Gorman's focus was on the nerve of Le Tour. Given his record, the man had to suspect he was being followed. And yet he had supposedly taken one of the most public forms of transportation available. Why not slip into the country via backroads? Or by boat?

Maybe he had, and they were running up and down this blasted train like the Keystone Cops for no reason. Maybe Le Tour himself had planted the rumor of the train to Edinburgh. He may have even gone so far as to plant some of the plastique on a couple of unsuspecting tourists, just to throw the authorities off, to divert their attention. A shell game.

The very idea brought on another wave of fatigue. Gorman wanted to give himself over to it, slip under and drown. They were running out of time. The announcement of their approach to the Edinburgh station had come.

He brought his tonic water to his lips, sincerely wishing it contained a good big shot of Bombay gin.

"Tired, luv?" Zuckerman asked, picture of the concerned girlfriend.

"Just contemplating murder," he said. "Charlie Roxbury had better be enjoying his vacation. It may be the last he takes."

"Think on the bright side, Neddie. When we catch this Le Tour bloke—and we will—you'll be the one getting promoted while Charlie's latest twit puts him through a wringer and turns him into steak tartare."

"She's MI5," Gorman pointed out.

Zuckerman sniffed in affront. "I know Melanie, luv. The number refers to her median intelligence."

"Meow."

She leaned toward him with a hand on his thigh. "I believe a real man prefers a real woman."

The fatigue vaporized. His eyes locked on hers. "I prefer a real woman."

Zuckerman smiled like the Cheshire cat. "See there?"

"And how are the lovebirds?" Franklin crowed, taking a seat across the small table.

Zuckerman smiled brilliantly. "You're such an ass, Thomas."

Gorman laughed. Under his breath he said, "Anything?"

Franklin shook his head almost imperceptibly. "Got near enough Gaspara *and* his luggage. Nothing on the E-nine. It's not him."

"Damn."

"Double damn. We'll be in the station in ten minutes."

"Let's sweep through again," Zuckerman suggested. "People will be milling about, gathering their belongings. No one will even notice us this time."

Gorman nodded, slipped an arm around her shoulders, and pulled her close, laying his head over on hers. Her breast pressed into his side. Nice. "We'll split up again. As the train's pulling in, if any of us have a likely candidate, we stick with them into the station. Agreed?"

The others nodded.

"See you at dinner then," Franklin said loudly, getting up from the table, then softly: "I'll take the front end."

Zuckerman leaned up as if to tell Gorman a secret. "You take my rear. Ooops! I meant the rear of the train." Drawing back, she gave him a playful wink. "For now, at least."

Gorman pulled in a deep breath as the adrenaline level rose again. He had to hitch a little at his trousers as he stood. His adrenaline wasn't all that was rising. Maybe he'd end up thanking Charlie Roxbury yet. Provided Le Tour didn't end up blowing half of Scotland—and most of the world's leaders—to kingdom come.

As Gorman made his way through car eight again, announcements rumbled over the train's speaker system. How to exit the train, where to pick up checked luggage, where to make connections. As Zuckerman had predicted, the attentions of their fellow travelers were focused on their arrival in Edinburgh, gathering children and belongings, chattering about the next leg of their journeys to wherever.

He checked the light on the E-9 every few minutes. Nothing. Nothing. Nothing. A sense of panic began to rise inside him. If either Le Tour or the plastique was on this train, they were about to lose their chance at it.

The train gave a bit of a lurch as it bent into a corner. He used it as an excuse to drop his carry-on next to a row of seats containing an athletic balding man in hiking gear and a tall, angular platinum blonde hugging a book bag and staring out the window.

Gorman apologized, bending down to retrieve the bag. The hiker gave him a vicious look. The woman glanced up at him with a vacant smile and a nod. She wore yellow-tinted rectangular glasses with thick black frames and was attractive in spite of them.

Discreetly, Gorman reached into the side pocket of the bag as the call came for all passengers to return to their seats. As he started to rise he was hit squarely from behind and knocked flat in the aisle. Before he could try to push up, the drunk who'd dropped him got tangled up in his feet and came down awkwardly on top of him. The breath went out of him in a whoosh. The E-9 went skittering under the seats.

"Get off!" Gorman grunted, trying without success to get his legs under him.

"'Xcuse me!" The breath the slurred words rode out on was heavy with the perfume of scotch. The drunk scrambled for purchase, digging his knee hard into Gorman's back, knocking him in the back of the head with an elbow.

"You'll have to return to your seats!" the conductor insisted, as if they were wrestling on the floor for the sheer enjoyment of it.

The drunk struggled up, staggering, stepping on Gorman's butt. "Shorry! I'm shorry. I really don't *like* trains," he drawled.

"Return to your seat, sir," the conductor said without sympathy.

Gorman remained on his hands and knees, staring beneath the seats. Where the hell had the E-9 landed?

"*Sir!*" the conductor snapped.

"Just a minute!" Gorman called. "I dropped something."

"You'll have to return to your seat."

"Hey!" the drunk shouted, suddenly truculent. "My friend said he *dropped* something!"

Heart pounding, Gorman spotted the business end of the sniffer. He dove for it, eliciting a shriek from a middle-aged woman in support hose and sensible shoes. She clocked him one over the head with a rolled-up magazine as he reached between her thick ankles to grab the thing.

"Sorry, ma'am! I'm really sorry," he said, scrambling backward. He pushed to his feet and slammed into the drunk.

"Hey!"

"*Take a seat!*" the conductor shouted.

Gorman fell into an empty seat, his ears ringing, his head pounding. He'd put his knee into something wet and sticky on the floor. None of it mattered as he turned the E-9 around.

The red light was glowing.

Oh Jesus.

They were coming into the station.

He looked around frantically at the faces. The sensible-shoes woman. A man who resembled Mr. Potato Head. A curly-haired child who stuck out his tongue. A businessman in a dark suit and sunglasses. The hiker.

Gorman's heart went into overdrive. They were coming into the station. Which one did he stick with? When had the bloody light gone on exactly?

The conductor was shoving the drunk toward the back of the car. Had the drunk seen the device and knocked him down because of it? Was the drunk a drunk at all?

He hit the reset button as the train screeched to a stop. The doors hissed open and the rush began. Everyone stood at once. People moved in a crush toward the doors, toward the luggage bins. Gorman started back toward the group of people he'd fallen past, openly watching for the light on the back of the E-9.

Mr. Potato Head: no.

Sensible Shoes: no.

He was jostled from behind and bumped into the hiker, who cursed him in French.

The collective mass of humanity surged toward the door.

French.

Le Tour was Belgian. The language of Belgium was French.

The blonde with the book bag and a couple of others had moved between him and the hiker.

The crowd was spilling out of the train and into the

station, where God knew how many people were rushing around.

The light on the back of the E-9 was blazing like an evil eye.

Gorman surged forward with the crowd, keeping his eyes on the hiker's bald spot. "Excuse me! Sorry!" he said, pushing his way through. The hiker looked back over his shoulder, scowling, turned around, and hustled on.

"Gotcha!" Gorman said under his breath. He lunged past Book Bag Woman, knocking her sideways, and reached for the hiker, catching him by the collar of his jacket. "FBI. Please step aside with me, sir."

The hiker tried to turn around and spit in his face, spewing a stream of virulent French. He jerked back around, dropped one shoulder, and was out of the coat and lunging through the crowd, backpack clutched by the straps in one hand.

Gorman swore and bolted after him, shouting, "FBI. Halt!"

The crowd parted like the Red Sea, the hiker shoving left and right, Gorman hot on his heels. He didn't even hear the shrieks and shouts. His focus was on Le Tour. Had to be Le Tour. He spoke French. He was running. The light had gone on.

It had to be Le Tour or Gorman's ass was grass with every superior from here to the Bureau chief.

Anticipating the hiker's move toward a side exit, Gorman cut the angle and dove for him, catching him tight around the hips. The hiker cried out and went down.

"You're under arrest!" Gorman shouted, tasting blood

as he scrambled to get a knee in the man's back. "It's all over, Le Tour."

"What's all that commotion?" asked the tall blond woman, staring back along the platform at the scene behind her.

The dowdy woman who'd been waiting for her arrival made a face of ferocious disapproval. "A drug fiend, I've no doubt. A decent person isn't safe to travel anywhere. Like as not, that train was full of drunkards and ruffians of all manner. The world is going to hell on a sled. Chaos all around."

"*Oui,*" the platinum blonde said in a sultry alto, shouldering her book bag. "And we must choose to be swept along by the storm, or to stand in the eye of it and control our destiny. No?"

Dowdy blue eyes gazed up at her with a sort of reverence and something more. "Aye."

They went out of the station and walked side by side across a parking lot; near enough to touch, but not touching. The air between them was charged with electricity. The blonde was elegant, tall, very chic in a slim, long black skirt, black tights, flat shoes, and a loose, long-sleeved tunic the color of slate.

"I've missed you," the short woman said almost under her breath.

"And I you, *cherie.*"

They neared a white VW microbus. The short woman unlocked the back door and they climbed inside.

They came together like a pair of thunderheads: violent, angry, hungry, wild. A tangle of tongues and lips and limbs, the clashing of teeth and passion. Clothes were pulled and torn and tossed. The layers of civilized facade came off one after another until they were naked—thigh to thigh, hips to hips, belly to belly, breast to chest.

The short woman lay back on the pile of clothes, naked, eyes as hot as blue flame. "Make love to me."

François Le Tour stared down at her—the wig and yellow-tinted glasses gone, lipstick smudged—filled with a passion for her that nearly matched the one he held for his cause. "I shall make love to you, my darling Sheena. And then we shall make war."

Gorman pressed a blue gel ice pack to his lip and glared at the hiker. Station security had descended on them and hauled them both off to a room in the labyrinth of administrative offices to sort out the mess. The hiker sat at the table, his lips curling with the kind of belligerent sneer that only French-speaking people ever truly master.

"I do not know what it is," he said contemptuously. "I do not know where it came from. I know only that it is not mine."

They all—the hiker, Gorman, the two security

93

guards, the police detective who had been called in—stared at the thing on the table. A matchbox from a restaurant in Brussels. But there were no matches inside. Plastique had been molded into the box. Enough to set off the E-9. They had torn apart the hiker's backpack and found no more explosive. A Ziploc bag of marijuana, yes. Plastique, no.

The cop started in again with the questions.

Gorman got up and went out of the room. Franklin and Zuckerman stood in the hall, Zuckerman smoking a cigarette and looking inappropriately serene.

"He claims not to know Le Tour," Gorman said. "I don't know. He could be telling the truth and just comes across like a lying asshole because he's French. Le Tour might have slipped the stuff in his pack when he wasn't looking. Or he may be a willing accomplice."

Zuckerman shrugged and blew out a stream of fine white smoke. "He looks the tree-hugging type. He's certainly got the attitude for a terrorist. That's more than I can say for mine."

Zuckerman's sniffer had gone red at the knitting bag of an older woman who had turned out to be a nun.

Franklin shrugged. He had zeroed in on a tourist with a golf bag and a twitchy look, but hadn't gotten a reading at all on his E-9.

Gorman swore and threw the ice pack against the wall, all of it overwhelming him at once: the jet lag, the frustration, the impatience. "We lost him."

"Well, there is an upside," Zuckerman said.

"We lost a man who's carrying around enough plastic explosive to level a few square blocks of this city," Gorman said angrily. "What could be the upside?"

"We know where he's going, ducky," she said, putting out the cigarette in a glass ashtray she'd pinched from someone's office. She set the ashtray on the floor, straightened, dusted her hands off, and smoothed her skirt. "Come along, Ned," she said, starting down the hall. "It's time for dinner, and I for one am famished."

"How can you eat that way, Ox?" Angus demanded. "We're on the brink of greatness here."

Ox might have looked up from his shepherd's pie, but his eyes were nearly invisible beneath his shaggy red brows. "Or the eve of disaster," he said and took another bite.

Angus went red. He leaned across the table, wild-eyed. "I'll not have you talk that way, Ox Ferguson!" He glanced around the pub for eavesdroppers and lowered his voice. "The world will know the name of Angus MacLout. The world will hear the story of the treachery of the MacGregors. And Phillip Bates will pay to see that it's done and that the wrongs are righted!"

Ox grunted and forked up another mouthful. Soft bits of potato dotted his beard.

Agitated, Angus sat back in his chair and drank half a glass of beer, his gaze constantly scanning the scene, as if he expected someone to leap up and point an accusatory finger at him. The pub was busy, full of smoke and noise and the smells of beer and food and sweat.

He himself stank, he knew. He was covered in dried

mud from digging half the day in a bloody trench to work on the golf course sprinkler system. Filthy job. And one that rankled mightily, having been assigned by Lorren Douglas, who was third cousin to the Mac-Gregors and knew full well the whole bitter tale.

Well, Lorren Douglas and his bloody cousins wouldn't be laughing after the end of this week.

He checked his watch. It was time.

He nodded to Ox and got up from the table. Ox stared down at the last few bites of his shepherd's pie, finally abandoning it. They wove their way through the mob and stepped out into the night air. The western horizon was still orange and pink, but lights glowed in the windows of the village that had hardly changed since the seventeenth century: narrow brick streets, tidy white-washed shop fronts.

They walked to the phone box on the corner, where a chunky girl with a cockscomb of dyed green hair was in the middle of an argument with someone on the other end of the line.

"I said no, Seamus! You never listen to me! That's half your problem . . . *Not listening!*" she shouted. "*That's* the problem!"

She looked out at Angus and rolled her eyes, then turned her back. "I know that's what you did, because Sheila bloody told me . . . I don't care she's a tramp. I know what she said is true."

"Bloody hell," Angus grumbled, checking his watch again. He stepped around to the other side of the phone box and glared at the girl. She gave him the finger and turned away again.

"You're a shit, that's what . . . Don't tell me to bugger off. *You* bugger off."

Angus came back around to the door of the box and knocked on the glass.

The girl stuck out her head. She had three nose rings and a silver bead below a lower lip painted black. "Bugger off!"

"You bugger off, little girl! I've got business to conduct on this telephone."

She looked him up and down and curled her lip. "Calling the pig farm, are you?"

"None of your bloody business!"

"This phone box is occupied," she said primly. "Use another."

"My associate is calling on *this* phone," he said. "*You* use another."

"Your *associate* is it?" she said snidely. "Well, you can tell your associate from me to *bugger off!*" She pulled back inside the box, shut the door, and leaned up hard against it.

Angus swore and pushed at it. Trying to move the little twit was like trying to budge a donkey. He banged at the door, kicked at it.

Ox stood by, inscrutable as a totem.

Angus turned to him at last, exasperated. "Will you bloody help me?"

"She's hung up."

The door opened and the girl came out and kicked him hard in the shin, square on the bruise Sheena had already left there. "You wasted all my time and me money ran out!" she cried, mascara running in dirty black streams down her pale cheeks. "You great stupid ass! You've ruined my life! I hope you're happy!" She kicked him in the other shin and ran away.

Angus howled, dancing from one sore leg to the other. He doubled over and grabbed at one shin, then the other. The phone rang and he banged his head trying to get in. He grabbed his head with one hand and clawed at the phone with the other, knocking the receiver off the hook. Out on the street, Ox just shook his head.

"Angus? Angus, are you there?" Sheena asked, brow knitting as she listened to the crashing on the other end of the line. She sat in bed in Edinburgh's Caledonian Hotel, swathed in rumpled sheets, her hair a mess.

"Sheena?"

"Aye. What's going on?"

"Nothing," Angus snapped. "Have you got what we need?"

"Aye. Picked it up a while ago."

"And where are you, then? Where is it?"

"Never you mind. It'll be there when you need it. You've the access we talked about?"

"Aye. Given over by kin of the MacGregors themselves. Ha! They'll know the wrath of the MacLouts! Vengeance is a dish best served cold!"

Sheena smiled at that, running a hand over her lover's chest. "Aye, Angus. That it is. I have to go now," she said as Le Tour reached for her breast. "We'll meet as planned. Try to keep out of trouble until then." She hung up as he tried to go on some more about the MacGregors and the time of reckoning.

"Your friend was not finished, *cherie*," Le Tour

pointed out, rubbing his thumb back and forth across her nipple.

"Angus never tires of his ranting. He's no doubt still talking, not having even noticed me hang up."

"What is this vengeance he seeks, *cherie*?" he asked, pulling back from her. He sat up enough to lounge against the mountain of fine down pillows. He'd made a lovely woman. He made an even lovelier man, with the body lines of an art model, the face of a wicked angel. "These Mac-Gregors did something to his family?"

Sheena sighed, already regretting the loss of the few minutes it would take for her to tell the ridiculous tale. "Two hundred years ago a MacLout bet a MacGregor his terrier could beat the MacGregor's terrier in a race. And he might have done if he hadn't leapt off course to attempt to breed a passing deerhound. MacLout—a drunken ass by all accounts—had bet Rathgarve.

"Angus believes the tale of his ancestors: that the MacGregors were responsible for the bitch in heat. The MacLouts claimed for two centuries the MacGregors were a crooked, cheating lot. And more than one MacLout lost life or limb in a duel because of it—them being terrible shots, drunk or sober. Angus believes that being the last of the MacLouts, Rathgarve is rightfully his, and therefore so is the money Phillip Bates paid for it.

"It's kind of like me saying that, as my name is Cameron—as is the fella who directed *Titanic*—that I'm entitled to a piece of the movie's profits. Do you think I should call him up, then?"

Le Tour chuckled deep in his throat, then slowly

sobered. "And this Angus will not create a problem for us?"

"Oh no, my love," Sheena cooed, sliding into his embrace. "I can take care of Angus. Don't you worry about that."

Chapter Four

NEVER UP, NEVER IN

by Lee K. Abbott

El Puma

Fernando Gaspara lay on the bed of his damp, cramped Edinburgh hotel room, staring dispiritedly at the water stains on the ceiling, waiting for the call that would tell him that the others had arrived, that soon their plans to show the world that El Puma had regained his former greatness could at last go into effect. Strange, he thought, as he listened to the incessant rain drumming on the gray windows, how those stains up there seemed laid out in the very map of Winged Foot. He'd been among the very best back then, he thought, suppressing a shudder. Now he was quite possibly the only person ever to have played the pro tour not invited to Phillip

Bates's tournament. Yet things would change. El Doctor had promised him.

Fernando felt another chill course through him, and he wrapped the musty bed quilt tight, his thoughts drifting back those few short weeks, to the day he had met the man who had undertaken this journey out of despair. The great, the terrible, El Doctor . . .

. . . by three o'clock Fernando Gaspara had forgotten how many times in the last hour he had checked the time—first on his Rolex, then on the timepiece in the shape of a human ear on El Doctor's desk. The appointment, he was sure, had been for two. On the dot, he'd been reminded only a few days earlier by what would turn out to be the disturbingly comely receptionist, a blonde with skin like mayonnaise and a voice on the phone that all but melted hair.

"The Doctor does not wait," she had said. "Waiting is for the hoi polloi. The serving class."

Fernando could appreciate that. He too was a busy man. Or rather, he had been a busy man. Before, of course, the advent of the Troubles. Those of a downright epochal sort.

"Only two weeks ago, President Bush was late. He had hoped to get his mind right, sharpen the edges, rid himself of a number of annoying rhetorical habits. His mind, sadly, remains wrong. Do we understand each other, Señor Gaspara?"

They did, he said, happily imagining a myriad of other understandings, each more delicious than its predecessor, they might reach together.

"We have other—what shall I call them?—rules, Señor Gaspara. For example—"

"*Por favor*," Fernando said, "call me Fernando. Or, better yet, El Puma. To the world I am the Puma, a sportsman of exceptional ferocity and daring."

She cleared her throat—as delightful a noise as he had heard that month.

"I'm afraid, Señor, that the Doctor has certain strictures against common informalities."

For an instant—as long, in fact, as it had taken in his golden olden days for a twenty-footer to hang on the lip before tumbling into the bottom of the cup—Fernando was crestfallen. First his game had deteriorated, and now even his legendary charm was turning sour. Then he reminded himself that he was El Puma, notorious for his recovery shots. A linkster no bush or whin or burn or swamp or bunker or waste area or rough could waylay. A caballero who at Winged Foot in '96, on the thirteenth hole, had played a shot out of the crotch of a tree to walk away with a par. And backhanded to boot!

"Strictures?" The word was as hard to get out of the mouth as was a three-putt to get out of the mind.

"We have a list of do's," she said. "And, not surprisingly, an even longer list of do not's. For example, you must never wear Ban-Lon. Or Sansabelt slacks. Pink is likewise a no-no."

"I, too, am opposed to pink. It is for girly-men. For the house pets of girly-men. For the women of Nueva Jersey—"

Again she cleared her throat, this time a sound with no delight in it whatsoever. "So we shall see you on Tuesday next, correct?"

Sí, he had said.

"At two o'clock," she had added. "Promptly."

And now here he was—had been, in fact, for over an hour. El sit-up-straight, mind-your-manners Puma. Apparently a schoolboy again. Yanked out of class and hustled to the assistant headmaster's office for a scolding, or a dozen swats on the tenderest tissues of his hindmost. He shifted in his chair, consulted his watch afresh. Ten minutes, he decided. He would give the doctor with all the strictures ten minutes. Then—oh, then, imperious as Caesar himself—one Fernando Gaspara would rise and exit, his chin high, his eyes dark with resolve.

He regarded his expression in the large mirror on the wall behind the desk. *Sí*, he was a handsome specimen. Hair slick as an otter's back, black and gleaming. The nose of a king. *Sí*, this was Fernando Maria Angel Gorostiza Miguel DeSoto Vasquez Pepito Garcia Colon Esperanza Gaspara: El Puma! The winner of seven majors. Four-time Ryder Cup veteran. Three-time winner of the Order of Merit. Holder of—

"A beverage, Señor Gaspara?"

It was the blonde, now standing in the door, hers a body that brought to mind the words "extirpation" and "thermocline." "A martini," he said. "Vodka, not gin. And a cocktail onion, if you please. A very small cocktail onion. In fact, put the onion on the counter next to the glass. Do not allow them—he-he-he—to get friendly."

Almost immediately she lifted her eyebrows, an

expression of infinite disapproval. Her eyes were almost glacial—brilliant blue orbs that, so it appeared to Gaspara, had seen everything this side of the moon at least once.

"A stricture?" he asked.

She nodded. So sorry, she explained. Rules were rules. In life as in golf. Without rules, only chaos. Goths loose in the streets. Catamites, perhaps. Even Tyuratum vertebrates. The potentialities boggled.

"A Pepsi?"

Alas, another stricture.

"Ginger ale?"

"Rule twenty-four dash six point seven, paragraph three," she said. "We're as particular about ours as the USGA is about its."

Fernando thought hard for a moment, a nearly herculean effort given the extraordinary distractions that were her thermoplastic go-go boots and a much bejeweled copper breastplate.

"A *cerveza* perhaps. Light."

Another rule, he learned, this from the darksome pages of the appendix.

"What then?" he asked, frustration growing.

She smiled, a despot with a new dungeon to populate. "Tonic water," she said. "An aid to digestion. A regimen of that—six weeks, say—and you'll have a lower bowel of stainless steel."

A second later she had turned, her hips doubtlessly on a swivel, and Gaspara, in his throat a heart swollen with desire, was about to follow when he suddenly felt against the nape of his neck a breeze as cold as that rising from the bottom of an ancient grave.

"El Puma, I presume."

The voice was like gravel in a bucket, Gaspara's moniker growing to a word no less than seven syllables in length. True, the Doctor had skin the color of week-old pork. And true, he seemed to be built like a toolbox. And yes, he was wearing a caftan and red ballet slippers. But Fernando sensed he would one day inform the *journalistas* from the world press that this Doctor would prove a miracle worker. A magician with everything but the wand and a top hat full of the continent's most endangered species.

"Have a seat, please," the Doctor said that day, a sentence about as sonorous as a train wreck. "You have a problem you wish to discuss, yes?"

For a moment, Gaspara studied the wall. On it were citations from the Tattooers of La Dominica and the Order of the Golden Dawn. On the desk sat a paperweight of a chimney from the college of cardinals. This was—gulp—embarrassing. Still, the Puma had come many miles and crossed many time zones to seek help from the greatest of sports psychologists—to the mind, so Bobby Stoops had put it, what Attila had been to the Huns.

"My game," he began, "it has—*Carumba!*—fallen apart."

"So I have read," the Doctor said. "The writer from *Golf World* called you a *renegado* and a hapless wight. You were likened to pestilence, I believe."

Gaspara shrugged with resignation. "And chemical warfare."

"Just so," the Doctor said.

"I am cursed," Gaspara complained. "At the Dubai Classic, Monty withdrew when my shadow fell on his shoes. My caddie, Humpy? He's taken to wearing Halloween masks. At Estoril in Portugal, he was Jesus of Nazareth."

The Doctor was taking notes now, his penmanship as tiny as crewelwork.

"At Bay Hill," Gaspara went on, hugely relieved to have someone to discuss his innermosts with, "the fans stood behind a Plexiglas wall. The official scorer wore body armor."

"I have read of the dark cloud over your head."

That was not all, Gaspara said. Not by a long shot. An exorcist had been dispatched from the Vatican. At the Peugeot Open de España, a marshal suffered a heart attack. In his locker, messages had begun to appear. "Abandon all hope ye who enter here." Tokens and talismans as well. India silk panties. A song had been written to ridicule him. An invitation to King Juan Carlos's polo party had been withdrawn. At the Hero Honda in Delhi, his courtesy car, good God, was to be a hearse.

The Doctor's hand sped across the page while Gaspara caught his breath. From the distance the clank of chains was reaching him. The air, he thought, smelled like brimstone.

"And your dreams?" the Doctor asked.

Terrifying, Gaspara said. In them a savage flitted in the trees, a being of lope and skinned knuckles. A bush prattled. In French. The earth shook. Fire poured down in waves. A dog in eye shadow and Princess Di's rubies.

"And your, uh, love life?"

Gaspara took note of his own hands. In his lap, they seemed to be locked in mortal combat.

"A standard question," the Doctor offered. "All is

related, you know. The yin and the yang. The alpha and the omega. The heart and the head."

Again Gaspara regarded hands. The left one seemed to have declared victory. "A true story," he said. "I am at a reception. As many dignitaries as—how do you say?—Carter once had Little Liver Pills. This is in Seville. A villa. I meet a woman. She is from the pages of a novel. Full-sprung thighs, a bosom to put an asp to. I approach. She has wet lips, the air around her special as blood. We converse. She is Sylvia, the daughter of a count from Slovenia. She is on holiday. She is delighted, may I say, to have made the acquaintance of El Puma, the Saracen of the Sweet Swing. I laugh. I am modest. I am in a tuxedo almost worth more than my first hacienda. I, too, am happy an acquaintance has been made. I take her hand. A charge passes between us. She is enthralled. I am hot with anticipation. Just then a waiter passes by. Champagne. Expensive champagne. More air than liquid. We toast, Sylvia and I. Passion, I am thinking, is imminent. Her gown is surgical gauze, held together by only a handful of threads. A pulse beats in her throat. I raise my glass. Her eyes twinkle. Only a moment, I think. And then—"

"You miss your mouth," the Doctor said.

Gaspara nodded. The champagne had dribbled down his shirtfront. It was one thing to whiff in the rough of the U.S. Open, he told the Doctor, quite another to shank one's own miserable *cabeza*.

For several moments the silence between them had both heft and hue. Gaspara remembered the lithe and luscious Sylvia virtually scampering away, snickering. El Puma? No, El Pollo was more like it. The Chicken.

"And now you seek my assistance," the Doctor said.

"I am at my wit's end," Gaspara allowed. "I stand on the tee and my legs wobble. The club will not wag. The ball has a mind of its own."

"You skull?"

Was the pope a Christian?

"You chili-dip?"

That too. Usually enough sod to carpet a hotel lobby.

"You top, I'm assuming."

Not only that, he also pulled and pushed and yanked and sliced and snarked and lopped and diddled and hotchopped and wizzled.

"The chunk is especially dispiriting."

Didn't compare to the foop. Talk about the slough of despond. The foop is to the chunk as the blowtorch is to the kitchen match.

"I am expensive," the Doctor said.

"I have money," Gaspara answered. "Reals, rupees, dinars, marks, pesos—you name it, I've got it. You want seashells and eyeteeth, you got them. The juice of nine Tanna leaves, the tears of an angel—anything."

"I am also demanding," the Doctor declared.

Gaspara had heard. The doctor had been compared to, among others, George S. Patton and Darth Vader. He was said to employ both thumbscrews and pliers.

"Failure is always possible," the Doctor continued. "No guarantees."

Right, Gaspara said. Ian Baker-Finch, Chip Beck, Corey Pavin. Failure was a given. Like sunrise. Because there was up, there was also down. No heights without depths. No Desi without Lucy. No Moby without Dick.

"First," the Doctor announced, "we must establish that you are a viable candidate for the program."

Gaspara took in the character of the office. In a word, spartan. A suitable situation for either a monk or an accountant named Meents. In addition to the desk and two chairs in the middle of the room, a plant stood in one corner. It could have been flesh once. Now it resembled a condition of being. Venery perhaps. Privation certainly. The Program, Fernando was sure, would be grueling.

"You have time," the Doctor said, "for some preliminary testing?"

"*Sí,*" he said. After a dozen consecutive missed cuts, enough bogeys to open a franchise, his birdies only those that soared in the heavens, and a lateral hazard last week at the Dutch Open in Hilversum that couldn't eat enough of his Maxflis, he had nothing but time.

"Excellent," the Doctor proclaimed. "We'll start with word association."

The first few, El Puma would forever remember, were exceedingly easy. Red? Why, the lips of Maria Elena Fernandez, Madrid's foremost flamenco dancer. Hot? The tramp of Tejas, of course, Rita Louise Shaughnessy. Interesting? Oh, a nun in a garter belt and stiletto heels. Fussy? Another gimme: the graybeards who ran the Masters. Warm? The breast of a woman named Sheena. Dark? *Madre mio*, the brow of the first ex-wife.

Love? The seventeenth at Congressional. Smooth? The haunch of Miss Teenage Toledo.

"Page two," the Doctor said.

Gaspara had rearranged himself in the chair. Already he felt better. Stronger. Keener of eye and ear. Focused. Time was falling away like old skin. The King? The Bear? The Walrus? Lefty and Boom-Boom and the Volcano and Long John and Jumbo—hah! *Atención*, los linksters! El damn Puma was on his way back!

"Insufflate," the Doctor said.

"New Etonics," Gaspara answered. "Black, with the stabilizer sole."

"Manchineel?"

Gaspara smiled. The air had never tasted as sweet. "A tropical euphorbiaceous shrub," he said.

The Doctor grunted, making a check mark on the topmost of a sheaf of papers as thick as the instructions for operating a solar system. "Palinode," he prompted.

Gaspara had to ruminate a second before answering.

"Use it in a sentence, please."

El Puma puffed himself up. The Program had become a stroll in high cotton. "Her palinodes made DL Three want to eat dirt."

At page four the Doctor had put on reading glasses. Now he was taking them off, his eyes lifeless as river rock. "Ethmoidal," he said.

Gaspara shuddered, his blood going cold and grainy around his lungs. His reply, scary as the spells a witch casts, had to be whispered. "The island green as Sawgrass."

For a moment, this long enough to be important, neither of them spoke. A darkness seemed to have descended. A wind had come up, steady and heavy with the stink of fear.

"Perhaps a libation," the Doctor said presently. "A meal maybe? I could have the chef whip up a dish or two."

Jesper had told him about the fare at the Doctor's. Ash, for starters. Tree bark. And garbanzo beans the size of bowling balls. The meat, he'd been told, was plywood. The outdoor grade.

"How am I doing?" Gaspara wondered.

The doctor sawed the air with his hands. The effect, Gaspara thought, was not unlike hearing your name called by Beelzebub. Or Moloch.

"You have a busy mind," the Doctor said softly. "I am thinking of a ferret in the trousers."

The blot test, the Doctor announced, would consume the better part of an hour. "Perhaps a short break," he said. "A rain delay, as it were."

Fernando thought not. He was ready now. He had stood over this sidehiller too long. It was time to putt or hit the showers.

"We are finding the parameters," the Doctor was saying. "It is my job to get the demons out of your head, to restore your confidence. I am to give you your macho back, your swagger. Twofold, if possible. If you are to swash anew, we must reinvigorate your buckle."

Fernando was taking an inventory of himself, especially the organs in outright revolt. "I am desperate," he said at last. "I have tried everything. The Shark's Secret. The Tempo Timer. The bullwhip shaft. Two days ago, to keep from looking up, I considered bolting a barbell to my forehead."

There was more, he said. He'd changed his grip, his stance. He addressed the ball as he would a rabid skunk. He'd tried new clubs, these alleged to be strengthened by an element the gringo astronauts had sneaked back from the moon.

"Patience, my friend," the Doctor said. "You have put yourself in the hands of a professional. I am to be your fakir, your shaman, your medicine man. We are trafficking in serious wampum here."

A word had occurred to El Puma, one composed of too many *X*'s and *C*'s to be used in polite company. In the mirror his reflection trembled on the verge of tears. "You spied on me," he said.

For a second the Doctor's face had an unlived-in aspect, an expression about as welcome as whooping cough.

"Behind the mirror," Fernando said, pointing to the wall. "You have a little room back there, no? While I waited, you watched. You were amused that I tried to work my wiles on your receptionist."

The Doctor smiled. Ten thousand of the most perfect teeth in the Northern Hemisphere. Then, evidently, he activated a switch hidden in his desk, for a door hissed opened behind him, revealing a room so dark and deep that Fernando believed virtually anything could now burst out of it. The furies themselves. Or the leggy tarts of the Moulin Rouge.

"I observed," the Doctor was saying. "It is a customary practice. I took notes. I do not judge. One does not judge the wind or a cloud."

Wind? Cloud? Gaspara looked around himself nervously. He had been likened to many things in his life, usually by his ex-wives—a snake's belly once, a vampire, the nightmare a worm has—but never the weather.

"You are a phenomenon," the Doctor said. "You are a mountaintop. Everest, say. Or a river. One does not condemn the Ganges for its riverness. Nor Pike's its peak. I am to reconnect you to your essential golfness."

Gaspara nodded. Of course. This was as reasonable as poetry.

"Your golfitude," the Doctor was saying. "Golficity. Golfation."

"I am a bird," Fernando suggested. "I must fly."

"*Exactamente*," the Doctor replied. "A toad must croak, mustn't it? And a toddler toddle? So must a duffer duff and a hacker hack."

Again Gaspara nodded, with growing enthusiasm. The sense here was so volatile he thought it might spontaneously combust. "You will restore me," he said, hopefully.

El Puma would be remanufactured, the Doctor explained. He would be broken down, disassembled, his parts cleaned and polished. His belts would be replaced, his gears reground. Psychologically speaking, of course. "At the appropriate hour," the Doctor concluded, "a swing guru will be brought in. I have a number on call . . ."

Gaspara shivered. Swing guru. The phrase had all the

appeal of a vacation in a Turkish prison. "How long will this take?" he asked.

The Doctor exercised elaborate care in straightening the paperwork around him. Something about the endeavor seemed to exhaust him. "How long do you have?"

Not long, El Puma said. He had to be in Scotland in less than a month.

"The Bates affair," the Doctor said.

Instantly and unaccountably, time seemed to be moving in three directions at once. The invitations—or in El Puma's case, the *non*-invitation—*had* supposedly been secret. Only the concerned parties, et cetera. So how—?

"I am a licensed sports psychologist, Fernando. Golf is my specialty. Little escapes my purview."

Now it was El Puma's turn to be tired. The day had been long. The first of many, he feared. A routine, he guessed, would be established. A new diet probably. No more gazpacho. No flan. No chimichangas. Porridge instead. Even gruel. Cross training too. No matter. It must be done. History was to be made there on Bates's magnificent course in Scotland. There El Puma would be resurrected.

"There is something else," he confided. "Another reason for haste."

The Doctor was studying his fingernails, an undertaking that seemed to require the concentration of a contract killer.

"Alfonzo Zamora," he said. "The Marvelous Mex."

An hour from this moment, El Puma would be describing what he saw in the ink blots. A cat's intestines in one. In another, a group of caddies playing strip poker. In a third, the shoes of a fisherman. An hour after that, he would be telling stories based on glossy pictures the Doctor had spread before him. A threesome of women engaged in rank carnality while their fiancés toiled on the practice tee. His papa weeping into his sangria. A cur pissing in a bowl his mother had made. But now El Puma was seeing nothing. Nothing except the greasy jowls of the living devil in a sombrero.

"I seek a grudge match," he told the Doctor. "He brings shame upon the Iberian heritage. He is a clown in the land of knights."

"He is Pancho," the Doctor said.

"And I am Cisco."

Fernando leaned forward. Declarations needed to be made. Points of view clarified.

"He is Cantinflas," he whispered.

"And you," the Doctor whispered back, "are Cervantes."

El Doctor

"And then you know what, Mrs. Sprague?" The Doctor was addressing his receptionist through the partially open door separating them. She was about to try on her fourth outfit of the evening. The shepherdess, the Doctor believed. An hour earlier, she had been a flight attendant, the transatlantic edition. Before that, a carpenter named Trixie—a carpenter with a full tool belt and a scarf joint to toy with. "Do you know what he said then?"

"I wasn't paying attention," she said. "I had Lumpy on the line. He needed more counsel. He was facing a pitch shot over a pot bunker on the tenth at St. Andrews. He hadn't moved in forty-five minutes." She chuckled, the laughter of Cleopatra herself. "That part of the booklet you gave him is in Persian. It computes using yods."

The Doctor took a moment for himself. On his CD system *Themes from Great Cities*, his favorite, was playing. This was cut four, "Islamabad," in particular the section where the Pakistani finger cymbals are meant to replicate an icy, almost providential rain. On the video monitor overhead he was watching Fernando Gaspara, El Puma, in his room, naked to the waist, rope in his fist.

"He was saying," the Doctor went on, "that he was upholding the honor of—what was his exact phrase?— the chippers of Chile and the putters of the Pampas."

"I know them," Mrs. Sprague said. "They can do handstands, too."

There was more, the Doctor said. On his way out of the office no more than three hours ago, El Puma had been declaring himself a crusader on behalf of Spanish bloodlines, the nobility of even the meanest. He was the toreador, Zamora but the lowly picador. El Puma was fine Corinthian leather, Zamora the squeaky "hide" of the cowardly Nauga. "Guess," El Puma had hollered, "who is the balata, who is the thing stuffed with goose feathers!"

"Shall I use the staff?" Mrs. Sprague stood in the doorway now, her hair styled by a tornado, hers the outfit sheep bleat for.

No, the Doctor sighed. Tonight would be staffless.

"Very good," she said. "Just one more minute. I need more straw."

On the monitor, noting that Fernando had begun his therapy, the Doctor turned up the volume.

"Forgive me, Señor Jones," El Puma was groaning, lashing himself twice on his bare back. "Deliver me, Ben Hogan. I am worthy only of your spikes." Again he struck himself, his lips curled in excruciating ecstasy. "I am begging your indulgence, old Tom Morris. I prostrate myself." The crack of the rope against El Puma's shoulders sounded like gunfire. "Harry Vardon, I seek only to carry your laundry. Perhaps a tip later on the backswing."

On the stereo "Addis Ababa" was playing now, it another melody equating volume with virtue.

"Mrs. Sprague," the Doctor called, "have you seen my address book?"

In his room, El Puma was asking for the forbearance of Messrs. Sarazen, Nelson, and Snead.

"Try the right-hand drawer," the receptionist called back. "It's beneath the *Hokmah*." It took him only a moment to locate it, scarcely another to find the number he was looking for.

"Who did we use last time?" he called again to Mrs. Sprague. "Motley or Cowboy Putt Fenno?"

Again Mrs. Sprague appeared in the doorway, fleece

slipping fetchingly free of one shoulder. Much about her posture suggested pain and transcendence. All she needed was a cudgel and a twenty-minute head start.

"Onan, I believe," she said. "Worked with that gorilla from the Australasian Tour. Bobby Stoops."

The Doctor thanked her.

"A maximum of two minutes, Doctor," she said. "I'm blackening my teeth."

While he dialed the number, he watched Fernando rise from and fall to the stone floor of his room at least five times. El Puma was up, hands clasped in prayer of the most abject sort, then he was down, whining like an abandoned puppy. His shoulders were beginning to redden nicely.

"This better be good," barked the voice on the phone. It sounded sixteen. Chinese, possibly. With a limp. "Cowboy Putt Fenno, please," the Doctor said.

"Who wants to know?"

No, eighteen. From the Dakota badlands. A south-paw. With, another tap-in, a tendency to lay it off at the top.

"Please tell Mr. Fenno that his meal ticket is about to be punched."

As a courtesy between colleagues, the Doctor had visited Fenno's ranch exactly once, a place in the track-less desert of loneliest New Mexico, south of a crossroad named—fittingly, the Doctor had decided—Lordsburg. About ten zillion miles from anything with a modern idea and the skill to use it. So far as the Doctor could tell, nothing was being raised there. Except gnarled flora and heat. Still, that's where Fenno, swing guru, had set up shop. It only made sense. You wanted to see

Moses, you went to where the seas had permanently parted.

"Tarnation, I'm about to sit down to my grub, Doc. What's got your mashie in the meatloaf?"

"Let me guess," the Doctor began. "Her name is, oh, Ida Lou, and she's playing Howdy to your Doody."

It took Putt Fenno nearly thirty seconds to stop laughing. "Her name is Florimel," he said at last. "And I'm tuning up her short game. Got the yips something spooky."

Now it was the Doctor's turn to ho-ho-ho. "I conclude, then, that you're in fine fettle this evening."

Putt Fenno snorted, sufficient decibels to occasion an avalanche in Switzerland. "What's my fettle got to do with a hog's affection for mud, Doc? I got fettle the way Congress has rascals."

"Belgrade" had come on now, the abbreviated version. Just enough so that you'd know, sooner rather than later, the difference between action and activity.

"Let's play a little game," the Doctor said. "A guessing game."

"Why in a ten-gallon chapeau would yours truly be interested in guessing any darn thing, Doc? I got about as many guesses as a gelding has lady friends."

"It involves money," the Doctor said. "A lot of it."

In the gulf between his words and Fenno's the Doctor heard what sounded like gristle. And, yes, a hinge creaking.

"Goldarnit, Doc, I don't need any more money. I got a filly here in buckskin and spurs about to giddyup her way into the LPGA!"

Putt Fenno liked the Doctor, not least because over the years the man had sent considerable repair work his way. Wanna-bes with swings that looked like the paths drunks followed falling down. Once a journeyman from the Japan tour with a swing so complicated it took him most of the morning to complete his preshot routine. You had to listen to a fellow, even a city slicker, that kept a steady stream of the halt and blind washing up against your chuck wagon.

"He's already called upon most of the saints," the Doctor was saying. "Leadbetter and Harmon. Pelz and MacLean. I figured it was time for the best."

"It's not Stankowski, is it? Sandals on the Tour? That's an affront to the game, Doc. A sin. And I won't abide it. Might as well pave over Pebble Beach, call up the folks at the Roller Derby and have done with the whole shebang."

Doc quite agreed. Sin was everywhere in the land. In the mulligan, for instance. And in the four-hundred-pound loose impediment.

"And not that Bates scallywag either," Putt said, only part of his attention devoted to the work of nature about to fit herself into the Swing Analyzer, a contraption that had arrived with more parables and metaphors than the Old dadgum Testament. "Bates was down here a year ago. Brought every blessed one of his sodbusters. A tenderfoot for each shoe, I swear. Wore the bonnet of a beekeeper, had a glove that could have been the skin of America's first virgin. Lordy, Doc, the Ephraimites could have lived out of his shag bag alone. Nicholson was with him, too. Kept snarling at the help. Miss Buckshot about soiled her pantaloons."

"You'll like this one, Putt. It's a total rehab. Wrist cock, follow-through, haircut, wave to the crowd."

Across the room, Florimel was working on her stance, an activity that, briefly, put Putt in mind of the sharpshooting talents of Lash LaRue and the Lone Ranger.

"I got a new curriculum, Doc. For a week, the client doesn't even touch a club. We do essay questions, fill in the blank. I got a fellow here right now still trying to figure out his first name."

From the Doctor's end of the line, Putt could hear music—most of it, as far as he was concerned, dangerously darn close to the soundtrack for the apocalypse itself. Like the clang of seven swords on seven shields or some such. The boom of a busted convenant. Maybe the bottom of high heaven letting go.

"It's Fernando Gaspara," the Doctor said. "El Puma himself."

Now Florimel was attending to her waggle, it as heartening to behold as a Roy Rogers fast draw.

"El Puddy-tat's more like it," Putt said. "What I saw at the One 2 One in Arden made me want to spit up."

Doc said he knew the feeling. Had you considering giving up membership in the human race.

"What was that thing he was doing with lips, anyway? That kind of behavior's illegal, ain't it? Hell, hereabouts you get arrested for even thinking the word 'petrous.'"

"I work on his mind," the Doctor said, "you work on his take-away."

For a moment, Cowboy Putt Fenno let the silence do all the talking. El Puma, huh? The mighty brought low, the meek bearing down fast on his fanny.

"This is the ultimate challenge." The Doctor sounded as excited as the last man scrambling for the last train bound for paradise. "You do this, you got nothing but pooh-bahs and pashas thereafter. And that's just the P-family of hackers. Wouldn't surprise me to see the whole Hooters and Nike tours come a-knocking. You know how good news travels."

Putt Fenno counted to himself. He didn't want to rush into anything. Last time he'd rushed in, he'd found himself with a one-iron in his hand, half of Death Valley to clear on the fly, and a buckboard of tinhorns present to applaud the effort. "What's that music?" he said at last.

The seaport of Pondicherry, the Doctor said. Putt was to ignore the Klaxons and sirens, not to mention the constant screams of terror.

"Mrs. Sprague, eh?"

"Little Bo Peep herself."

Putt spent the next several seconds reflecting upon his circumstances. A practice tee full of folks paying a thousand greenbacks a week to get their bushes whacked and their sores saddled, golfwise speaking. A catalog called *Fenno's Fairways*, which sold memorabilia and learning aids, including a shirt that kept score, and *Cowboy Putt to Nirvana*, a series of inspirational videos that featured his staff of seventeen and the voices of the Sagebrush Sisters of Sacramento doing backup. And, yes, across the room a thoroughbred linkster with a swing of nearly gunslinger specifications.

"Okay," Putt said. "Get him here in two days."

"Two days?" the Doctor sputtered. "But he and I can be there tomorrow."

Putt took a deep breath. Something tight was snapping loose in his gut bucket. He felt he was in the circus again.

"Tomorrow, Doc, Sister Florimel here will be perfecting her ability to pronate."

At precisely the gong of midnight, Mrs. Sprague threw open the door to the dressing room and stepped into the shadows of what the Doctor referred to as his Theater of Possibility. Oddly, she'd been thinking about Billy, that knucklehead, trying to remember how many years had passed since she'd fled Squat Possum and the endless yakety-yak about niblicks and spoons and divot repair tools, never mind all that *Little Pink Book* hokum that creepy Earle Toland spewed forth. Geez, you'd have thought the geezer was Professor Aristotle himself. "Life is a chip shot from the froghair of fortune." Cripes, what the dickens did that mean?

"Billy on the brain again, eh?"

It was the Doctor, his body seeming to have absorbed virtually all the light in the room. Nowadays she believed him to be as much in her head as out.

"Strange, isn't it?" she said. "Months can go by and I

barely remember him. Then—poof—I'm seeing that freckled back going into the shower."

"It's the ions," the Doctor said. "A change in barometric pressure. An aberration in liver function, a drop in the blood sugar perhaps."

She stood beside him now. He was on his stomach, face turned away from her. His caftan, big as a mainsail, lay on the floor in a heap. His slippers, she supposed, were outside the security door. With his hairpiece. And his teeth.

"You smell delicious tonight, Mrs. Sprague."

"It's an ointment," she said. "A gift from Miss Shaughnessy. Before, of course, that business with the Nabisco people. The ingredients are in Norse."

She spent a minute gazing at the closed-circuit monitor mounted near the ceiling in the far corner. Señor Gaspara was asleep, his burlap bedclothes twisted around his legs. His dreams appeared to concern long-distance swimming. In a pool of piranha.

"He didn't eat his bean," she remarked.

"True," the Doctor said. "But most of the mulch is gone."

Time seemed to move ahead in spasms and jerks. In a moment or two, she knew, they would commence. The sequence had been established early on, less than a year after her discharge from the marine corps, where she'd fled for surcease after Billy. All had once been familiar, comforting. The gestures. The dialogue. The heave of the heart. But now? Well, how had that stupid book put it? "Now is a pin placement on the green of then." Sheesh.

"Daisy," he was saying. "That's such a pretty name."

It had been her granny's. The shrew.

"Tell me, Daisy," the Doctor began, "have you ever been to Scotland?"

"Isn't that where they play golf?"

He smiled at her. "Why is it that you don't like golf?"

Her fingertips rested on his flank now. It felt like a truck fender.

"Oh, I don't mind golf," she said. "It's golfers who drive me crazy."

Chapter Five

TIGHT LIES

by Tim O'Brien

Billy Sprague, Alfonzo Zamora, and Rita Shaughnessy were among the first guests to arrive at Rathgarve Castle. It was a drizzly, forlorn afternoon—Scotland's finest weather in months.

At the registration desk, as they were checking in, Rita gave Billy Sprague a sharp nudge in the ribs. "Hey, stud," she whispered. "Over there. Isn't that—you know—isn't that Bob Hope?"

"Where?" said Billy.

"By the fireplace."

"The guy with the frizzy beard?"

"No, silly, that's the pope." Rita made a pointing motion with her breasts. "Over there. On the sofa."

"The dead one?"

"He's *dozing*."

Billy whistled. "Bob Hope! I guess this *is* a big deal."

Alfonzo Zamora snorted and wagged his head. "Yeah, it's Hope all right, but don't get yourself all in a lather. I played with him once at Pebble, that pro-am nonsense. Dude couldn't hit a green with his own nose and a bombardier. If it's talent you want, take a gander over at the elevators."

"Billy Joel!" said Rita.

"That is *not* Billy Joel," said Alfonzo.

"Well, hey, it sure as heck looks like—"

"Matt Lauer. Dirty sandbagger took a hundred bucks off me in Gumbel's tournament last year. Twelve handicap, my ass."

Rita laughed. "What'd you do, play him with that taped-up Pepsi bottle of yours?"

"No, the guy just happened to—"

"Or maybe you pulled out that *other* stubby club of yours? I mean, no wonder you got clipped."

Alfonzo saw not the slightest humor in this. He was still suffering from the aftershocks of the attack on his cranium back in London. Rita had found him on the floor of her hotel room, semiconscious, muttering to himself, a divot the size of a prayer rug carved out of the back of his skull. He still had no idea who—or exactly what—had hit him. A sand wedge, maybe. Possibly a nine-iron. In any case, he was feeling wobbly. His vision, which had been deteriorating for some time, had now taken a decided turn for the worse.

He blinked and glanced back at the elevators. Christ, maybe it was Billy Joel. Or Bill Murray. A guy in knickers, that much for sure.

Almost for sure.

"Hey, daydreamer!" Rita snapped. "Here's the program. Let's hit the showers, freshen up, then meet at the first tee for a quick nine holes. Get in a warm-up round."

"Sounds fun," said Billy. "Just a friendly game, right?"

"You betcha," Rita said. She swatted him on the rear. "In your case, stud, real *extra* friendly."

Alfonzo shook his head. "Count me out. Some sleep, that's all I need. About eight hours of sack time." He shot Rita a wink. "You're always welcome, naturally."

"Naturally," Rita said. For a moment it looked as if she were about to slug him, but then she grinned and flicked her eyebrows. "Tell you what, Alfie. I'll golf you for it."

"Say again?"

"You heard me. Nine holes. Match play. If by some once-in-a-zillion fluke you beat me, you get to play a tenth hole."

"Tenth?"

"Luscious dogleg, the boys tell me."

Alfonzo squinted. "Yeah? What's the hitch?"

"No hitch," said Rita.

Billy Sprague gave Rita a disapproving frown. "Well, gosh. I'm not so sure I go for this. I thought you and I were sort of a pair now. Playing partners."

"Oh, we are," Rita cooed. "That's what I meant by freshening up."

"Then why—?"

"Teach this fat Mex a lesson, that's all."

The three of them made their way toward the elevators. Already the lobby was beginning to fill up with celebrities of all stripe and station. Phillip Bates had just strolled in with the prince of Wales; Madonna was showing off her new lob wedge to Fidel Castro and Hale Irwin, while over near the bellhop stand, deep in conversation, were Ken Venturi, Augusto Pinochet, and Bob Costas.

Rita punched the elevator's up button. "Now here's the deal," she said. "If I beat you, Alfie—about which there is absolutely no doubt—then I never hear another sex-Mex comment out of you. No more bragging. No more come-ons."

"Yeah?"

"Plus a thousand bucks."

Alfonzo took a short step backward. "Let's get this straight. Match play, nine holes. You win, I shell out a thousand clams. I win, all I get is laid?"

"Exactly."

"You must be nuts."

"Are we on?"

"On," Alfonzo said, and giggled. "You bet your sweet ass."

Upstairs, Billy and Rita finished their lovemaking in record time, the lowest stroke total ever recorded on Rita's much-played public course.

"Now that," said Rita, "was a pick-me-up."

Billy nodded. The last stroke had been a gimme—a nine-incher at most—but even so he'd come close to blowing it. Story of his life.

"Very nice," he said, then paused and cleared his throat. Rita's wager was still bothering him. "Listen, you aren't

serious about playing Alfonzo for—you know—for sex?
A joke, right?"

Rita shrugged her formidable shoulders, farted, slipped
out of bed, and lit up a Winston 100. "No sweat, tiger,"
she said. "Don't worry about it. I could whip that greasy
has-been with a Wiffle ball and a set of trainer Spald-
ings."

"Yes, but—"

"But what?" she said. "You aren't getting possessive, are
you?"

"Of course not."

Rita turned and looked down at him. "Because, sweetheart, here's the straight scoop. You and I just met."

"True."

"Well, there we are then. Besides, I'm my own woman,
captain of my vessel, all that good stuff." She paused.
"You're a nice guy, Billy, but I'm not into property rights."

Billy watched her march off toward the bathroom.

Lovely creature, he thought. But it wasn't a question of
property rights. No way on earth.

Just love.

Twenty minutes later, Rita and Billy and Alfonzo—sans
Hector, laid up in his Rathgarve rollaway with a combination of jet lag, head cold, and dread—stood under their
umbrellas on the first tee. It was late afternoon, nearly
three-thirty, and the day's drizzle had become a full-

fledged rain. The unseasonably superb weather was holding.

On an adjacent putting green, also under umbrellas, mingled such notables as Tony Blair and Al Gore, both decked out in tweeds and starched golf shirts. Nearby, Mu'ammar Qaddafi was giving a now-or-never, sink-it-before-you-die putting lesson to Jack Lemmon, while only a few feet away Chi Chi Rodriguez did his best to adjust the clumsy, rather primitive one-handed putting stroke of former senator Robert Dole.

"So what's the batting order?" Alfonzo asked. He glanced at Rita, bowed from the waist, and issued a taunting chuckle. "You plan to hit from the ladies' tee?"

Rita smiled. She put down her umbrella, strolled forward, teed up a scarred old Titleist, and whacked it two-eighty down the center. "Ho-hum," she said.

Alfonzo glanced over at Billy Sprague. "Not bad," he grunted. "The tramp put both hams into that one."

"Be polite," Billy warned.

"Hey, amigo. That was polite."

Billy went next. He felt like a third wheel—along for the ride, no pressure at all, nothing at stake—and his drive sailed a good ten yards past Rita's.

"Side wager?" Alfonzo said.

Billy shook his head. "No thanks. I'm not a betting man."

"So I hear."

Alfonzo cackled at this. He waddled up to the tee box, took a quick look down the fairway, then ripped off his patented high fade, a truly gorgeous drive that seemed to find its own air currents before settling down well past Billy's ball.

"Shit-a-rino," he muttered. "Shanked it."

Then he cackled again.

Their Scottish caddies hefted up the bags and began heading down the fairway, but after only a moment or two there was a loud huffing noise behind them. It was Bob Dole. He wished to join them.

For a few seconds Alfonzo pretended not to notice. He picked his teeth with a tee, stared off into the rain. "Jeez, Senator, I don't know," he finally said. "Is it contagious?"

Dole scowled. "Is what contagious?"

"Well, you know, that business on TV. That disease. I forget what you call it."

"Erectile dysfunction?"

"Yeah, right. No offense, my man, but . . . See, I've always played with pretty stiff shafts, if you follow my drift. Super stiff, actually."

"Listen, you fat little—"

Rita and Billy separated them.

"Okay, okay," Alfonzo growled. "Let the guy tag along. One thing I can't stand, it's a pissed-off Republican." He thrust out a conciliatory right hand toward Dole. "Forget I said a word. Shake on it."

As it turned out, however, the former GOP standard-bearer returned to the clubhouse midway down the first fairway. (In part, no doubt, his departure had to do with Alfonzo's running commentary about the senator's "weak grip," how he should "give some serious thought to working on that handicap.")

Watching Dole stalk off into the rain, Alfonzo shook his head sadly. "There goes one dude," he said, "who most definitely keeps his head down."

Alfonzo won the first hole with a tap-in birdie. Rita captured the second hole, a two-hundred-thirty-yard par-three, with her own slick little birdie.

It went back and forth that way, no real blood, and after five holes the match stood dead even. Both Rita and Alfonzo played well, collecting their pars, bearing down, focusing on each shot. Nothing fancy. No risks, no mistakes. The really brilliant play, though, came from Billy Sprague, who birdied five straight holes effortlessly, his swing as graceful as a panther on the prowl. For Billy, the game of golf had little to do with mechanics, even less to do with wagers or competition. Golf was man-in-nature. It was wind and rain. It was grass. It was the flap of the flag, the earth beneath his feet, the flex in his knees as he addressed a tough sidehill lie.

Watching the match between Alfonzo and Rita—the cussing, the elation, the tension, the relentless ups and downs—Billy Sprague felt a deepening melancholy. This, he thought, was a corruption not only of golf, but also of the human spirit. Playing for sex—playing for anything beyond the pure joy of playing—struck him as the next closest thing to blasphemy.

Besides, he loved her.

Yes, he did.

And his heart was breaking.

Rita eagled the sixth hole, a long and very difficult par-five, to go one up. Alfonzo immediately replied with a birdie on the seventh. Again, the match was square, but for Billy Sprague the world was not so square: the world was fucked up.

It mattered nothing to him that his own score now stood at seven under, that he was playing the best golf of his life.

On a rise overlooking the eighth green, in the gloom and steady rain, Ned Gorman looked on through a pair of binoculars. At his side was a decidedly soggy Edna Zuckerman.

"What the hell's happening?" she said.

"They're all even," Ned said.

"I don't mean that! I mean, why the fuck are we out here in the first place? I'm drenched, I've got a fucking head cold. Besides, I fucking hate this fucking game!"

Ned smiled and stared through the binoculars. "It's a job, honey."

"Job how? What's the point?"

Ned kept his eyes locked on Rita Shaughnessy as she stood over a ticklish five-footer. Quietly, for the hundredth time, he explained that they needed to get the lay of the land, that a terrorist might well be lurking in any bramble bush or bunker or patch of gorse. "The tournament officially kicks off tomorrow," he said patiently, "and we've got to know this place—the whole layout—the way a farmer knows his back forty. Like I say, it's our job, baby." He leaned forward and squinted into the binoculars. "Besides, one of those three idiots could be our man. Or woman. Depending."

Edna yelped. "But I'm *freezing*!"

"Well, you never know, pumpkin. Anybody crazy enough to play in weather like this . . ."

"Of course they're crazy! They're *golfers*, for chrissake." She shivered and hugged herself. "And don't call me fucking *pumpkin*!"

"Shhhh."

"Shhhh what?"

"The Shaughnessy woman's putting. Pipe down. Try to show some manners."

Down on the eighth green, as Rita stroked her putt, Edna Zuckerman's angry scream pierced the gloom.

"Scuffed it, huh?" said Alfonzo.

"That wasn't fair!"

"Sorry, señorita. I guess them's the breaks."

"Well, sure, but—"

"No mulligans."

And thus, as the waterlogged threesome trudged toward the ninth and final tee box, Rita Shaughnessy was one down and in deep trouble.

Billy Sprague was eight under and heartsick.

Alfonzo Zamora was one up and cackling.

And Ned Gorman was lecturing Edna Zuckerman on issues of golf etiquette. And getting nowhere.

"Well now, here we be," said Alfonzo. He was beaming, flush with confidence, gazing serenely at the short par-three ninth hole below them. The green lay at the bottom of a deep gorge, which was now partly shrouded in fog and rain. "Way I figure it, Rita, the best you can hope for is a tie. Best I can hope for is that famous tenth hole of yours." He grinned. "Tight fairways, as I recall. Lots of cleat marks around the cup."

"Watch your language," said Rita. "And don't start counting unhatched chickens."

"Cock-a-doodle-doo!" said Alfonzo.

Billy Sprague said nothing.

It was nearly dark now. The famous gloaming had set in, bewitching hour, and the relentless rain gave the course a dismal, deserted, even forbidding aspect. A mass of bloated, purply-blue clouds seemed to press down upon the earth; the heather along the tee box had the look of mutant seaweed, and a deep pot bunker in front of the green had filled with enough rainwater to house Nessie and her brood. And that was just the start of it.

Over the last half hour the temperature had dropped to just above freezing. Gale force winds knifed in from the North Sea, whipping sleet across the course, and shards of hoarfrost clung to Alfonzo Zamora's super-stiff titanium shafts. ("Difficult conditions," Ken Venturi might well have commented to a television audience, had he not been warming himself before a roaring fire back at the hotel. Indeed, even the caddies had abandoned them more than an hour ago, somewhere along the third fairway. ("Ill bodings, lads and lassies," one of them had squealed, and then scampered away into the dark.) For ordinary souls, in other words, here was the biblical prototype of hell. But for the true golfer—certainly for Billy Sprague and Rita Shaughnessy and Alfonzo Zamora—it was also the purest heaven.

"Your honors," said Rita.

"Ladies first," said the courtly (and now very cocky) Alfonzo. "I insist."

"Do you?"

"I do."

Rita shrugged. She teed up her old Titleist, stood back, and surveyed the shot.

Unlike most championship par-threes, the ninth was laid out in a very short, very simple configuration—a modest hundred and forty-two yards from tee to green. Much of it straight downhill. No water. No rough. Just a lonely-looking pot bunker fronting the green. To a professional eye, however, the green's steep back-to-front slope presented trouble. Like a great funnel, the entire front of the green was little more than a giant ball collector running downward into that innocuous pot bunker.

Anything short of pin-high, Rita realized, and you were dead.

She pulled out her nine-iron, paused a moment, then changed her mind in favor of an eight. Then the nine again. Then the eight. Then her wedge. Then back to the nine.

"Jesus Christ," Alfonzo moaned. "It's like watching my ex-wife in a boutique. Choose your weapon, for God's sake."

"Tough wind," Billy murmured.

"Not *that* tough."

"Pretty tough, though."

Rita eventually settled on the nine-iron. Which was unfortunate.

As always, her swing was flawless—nerves of platinum, Billy thought—and the ball screamed high into the rain, dead-on at the flag, disappearing for a few seconds, then reappearing as it dropped onto the green two feet short of perfect. The ball bit like a police dog. It jumped backward, seemed to hesitate for an instant, then wobbled and caught the slope and began a slow, torturous, deadly trickle toward the pot bunker in front of the green. "Oh shit," Rita muttered. Slowly at first, then rapidly, the old Titleist journeyed ten, twenty, thirty, forty yards, finally plopping into the deep bunker.

Start to finish, the shot consumed a good three and a half minutes of play time. (In a sanctioned PGA tournament, the entire threesome would have been disqualified for slow play.)

"Well," Alfonzo said, and feigned a sigh. "Guess you should've grabbed that ol' eight-iron, right?"

"Right," Rita mumbled.

"Next time don't be so rash. You got to think things over. Like my ex-wife, sort of." Alfonzo cackled his irritating cackle. He strode quickly onto the tee box, took a single practice swing, and then cracked a perfect eight-iron high into the clouds. He stood waiting.

For a long, long while he waited. The ball seemed to have been swallowed by the clouds.

Alfonzo finally turned. "Anybody spot it?"

"Spot what?" said Rita.

"My ball. All this fog and rain—these fucked-up eyes of mine—I couldn't see the damn thing come down."

Rita rolled her shoulders.

"Probably on the green somewhere," Alfonzo said. "Maybe in the friggin' hole."

"Yeah, maybe," Billy Sprague said. "Or else lost."

"Bullshit."

"Hard to tell," Billy said. "The thing to do, I guess, is hit a provisional."

"On a par-three?"

"Just in case."

Scowling, talking to himself, Alfonzo teed up for the second time. Once again he rifled a lovely eight-iron high into the clouds; once again he waited; and once again the ball did not reappear.

"That's it!" he yelped. "No more provisionals. One of them two babies has got to be safe."

Immediately, without waiting for Billy to hit, Alfonzo hoisted his bag and waddled off rapidly into the gorge, heading for the green. Within seconds he had vanished into the heavy weather.

"Your turn," Rita said.

"Forget it," said Billy. "I'll just pick up and watch you two slug it out."

"You're eight under, man."

Billy shook his head. "It's not the score, it's the game."

"Stuff the metaphysical Michael Murphy crap."

"Seriously. I'm done for the day."

Rita studied him for a long, disbelieving moment. "Shit, man, no wonder you never made it as a pro. You're just too damn pure, Billy. Too damn noble. At least for this gal."

Then she followed Alfonzo into the rain.

For a few seconds Billy stood alone on the tee box. The day's bleakness had now seeped into his heart. Too pure, he thought. Such nonsense. The sad truth, of course, was precisely the reverse: the pressure had been too much for him. He was a quitter—terrified of collapsing on the final hole. Terrified of ruining a perfect round of golf.

He nearly wept.

When Billy finally trudged up to the ninth green, Alfonzo Zamora was still scouring the landscape for his two missing balls. Nothing on the green. Nothing on the fringe. And the cup, too, was empty.

Rita tapped her wristwatch. "Your five minutes is almost up," she said. "Two lost balls."

"Yeah, but it's not fair!" yelled Alfonzo. "My damned eyesight."

"Real pity. Like somebody just told me, them's the breaks. Go hit another one."

"Forget it. Those balls are here somewhere."

At that instant, just off the left fringe of the green, Billy Sprague spotted a dull glint of white. He looked away, took a breath, then looked back again. The ball lay under a bit of blown heather, almost entirely obscured, not twenty feet from the pin. Imprinted across the dimples were the letters AZ—it was Zamora's all right. Almost certainly his original drive.

Billy stood paralyzed for a time. To speak up, he realized, would be to hand the match to Alfonzo; he might just as well escort Rita to the man's bed. And the image of their lovemaking was intolerable to him. He couldn't help but picture the moist suction at their bellies, Rita's eyeballs rolling toward the ceiling.

Billy glanced down at the ball, then up at the heavens, then back at the ball again. Silence, he tried to tell himself, was not cheating. He was a spectator after all, and nothing in the rule book required members of the gallery to point out lost balls.

Even so, deep in Billy's golfing heart it somehow felt like cheating.

Briefly he looked over at Rita, who stood watching him from near the deep pot bunker. Maybe she too had spotted the ball. Or maybe not. Either way, her eyes seemed to bore in on him, partly in mockery, partly challenging, partly as if to ask a single devastating question: Which will it be—love or honor?

Billy closed his eyes. The moral tug-of-war was ripping his heart in half.

"Over here," he said quietly.

Alfonzo Zamora spun around. "Say what?"

"Your ball. Right here."

There was a moment of immense quiet—even the rain went silent—and then Rita shook her head and spat and turned away.

Alfonzo hustled over to his ball.

"Numero uno!" he crowed. "I'm lying one. Looks like it's all over but the fuckin'!"

For Billy Sprague, whose heart had gone brittle, the next several minutes were little more than a blur. He watched Rita disappear into the deep pot bunker. A moment later, in a great splash of sand and water, she managed to hoist her scarred old Titleist onto the green— but still thirty-five feet from the cup. Alfonzo chipped to within two feet.

Something sparkled in Zamora's eyes. Confidence, maybe. Or maybe greed.

"All right, señorita, I tell you what," he said and grinned at Rita. "Double or nothing."

"Sorry?"

"Very simple. If you make that putt, babe, we're all even. No blood spilled. Even-steven. Miss it, though, and you owe me a whole week's worth of hay time. Plus two thousand bucks."

Rita's eyes narrowed.

She looked over the thirty-five-footer, pulled a flask from her hip pocket, took a quick nip, and then slowly nodded.

"You're on," she murmured.

"Except there's one little catch," Alfonzo said.

"What's that?"

"Billy putts it for you."

"Billy? No way. The guy couldn't sink a clutch six-*incher.*"

"Take it or leave it," Alfonzo purred.

And there it was again: that greedy sparkle in his eyes.

Rita sighed. "Oh, well," she groaned. "No choice, I guess."

Billy was already striding off the green—trotting, in fact—when Rita snatched him by the neck and squeezed hard.

"Mister Integrity," she snapped. "You got me into this pickle, now get me out. Show some guts."

"Look, I'm just not—"

"Do it."

"But I *can't*," Billy whimpered. "I swear to God, if I hit that putt, it'll end up in Glasgow. Or maybe Aberdeen. You never know."

He tried to wiggle away, but Rita still had him firmly by the neck. She marched him across the green, squared him over the ball, and forced her putter into his hands.

"Just roll it home," she said. "Nice and smooth. And don't forget, my virtue is at stake."

"You don't *have* any virtue."

"Totally beside the point."

"Yes, but—"

"Run that putt in, Billy, and all's forgiven. Even the Michael Murphy crap." She gave him an encouraging pat on the butt. "Come on, now, you can do it."

Then she released him and stepped back.

Billy's world went topsy-turvy. For a good three minutes he hovered over the putt, trying to steady himself. His whole body was shaking—everything— arms, fingers, knees, brains. His head buzzed with evil memories. A whiffed six-iron back in junior high, a yanked drive in his first club tournament, a three-foot putt that sailed out of bounds on the final hole of an exhibition match in Sioux City.

Billy closed his eyes. There was no point, he realized, in trying to read the green, or lining up the putt, or even taking aim.

Blindly, with a short, plaintive moan, Billy took a desperate stab at it.

The ball jumped off the putter as if launched by NASA. For the first thirty feet, the old Titleist did not touch the earth, heading for orbit, engines roaring, but then suddenly the rain and wind and fog forced a scrubbed mission. Gravity reasserted itself. By pure chance—a miracle, some would call it—the ball dropped heavily onto the green, not five feet from the cup. When Billy opened his eyes, he was stunned to see Rita's beat-up old Titleist rolling gently holeward. Incredible, he thought, but the putt actually had a chance. It caught a sidehill slope. It wobbled off line for a second, then straightened out and continued its erratic pilgrimage toward destiny.

Rita let out a whoop.

Alfonzo uttered a cussword that would be cause for lethal injection in the state of Texas.

The ball was now four feet from the cup.

Three feet.

Two feet.

Then it came to a complete halt, six inches short. For a few seconds nothing more happened—so close, Billy thought—but after a time the old Titleist seemed to suck in a breath of air, recharging itself, igniting its boosters. The ball took another half turn. Then another. As it approached the lip of the cup, still rolling, Billy released a cry of simple joy. All those years of frustration.

Then the scarred old Titleist exploded.

First came a flash of yellow, succeeded by bright orange, succeeded by a shock wave that blew Billy backward. Alfonzo was picked up, carried skyward, and then dumped back to earth like a family-size bag of tortilla chips. Rita lay face-up on the green.

Where the cup had once been, there was now a yawning six-foot-wide crater.

After a moment Alfonzo dusted himself off.

"Now there," he said quietly, "is one spectacular case of the pressure-yips."

Chapter Six

IMMOVABLE OBSTRUCTIONS

by Richard Bausch

Ned Gorman and Edna Zuckerman had made their way through the rain and mist, the dripping trees, to the road, and then got in the car, soaking wet and shivering, and drove to the castle. Neither of them looked at each other. She was angry, sulking. "It was one of those trick balls," he said. "I've seen it before. You buy them in the novelty shops. This one had been beefed up a little, but any twelve-year-old can do it."

"You don't think it had anything to do with our boy."

"I'd be very surprised if it did. And for Franklin to come running out there from the clubhouse, like the goddamn U.S. Cavalry—well. We're gonna have hell now, because Le Tour, if he's here—and he's here, you can bet on it—knows *we're* here too, now."

"Tom could have seemed a course official. It *was* an

explosion, after all. It didn't look like anyone was seriously hurt. They were all standing around afterwards."

"That putt was in the hole, too."

She said nothing for a moment. "Why would it have to be the U.S. Cavalry?"

"I don't know."

"That's the way it is for you Americans, isn't it? The whole bloody world revolves around you. I can't tell you how tired I am, for instance, of your fucking Civil War, like nobody else ever had one. We had one that lasted a hundred years for Christ's bloody sake."

"They just call it the Hundred Years War. It didn't really last a hundred years."

"It lasted longer than yours. It was bigger than yours."

"Okay," Ned Gorman said. "I don't have a problem with that."

"We're not negotiating."

"Look," he said. "What's got into you? We watch a little golf and suddenly you're Margaret Thatcher."

They had come into the parking lot of the castle, and as he spoke, the former prime minister loomed up on his left, waiting to step out into the lot. She was wearing a clear plastic raincoat and was holding an umbrella herself, and was alone, but it was Margaret Thatcher.

"You saw her," Edna Zuckerman said.

"I swear I didn't," said Gorman. "Not until after I'd said it."

"Well, it makes no difference."

"I'd like credit for the remark."

Edna Zuckerman was staring at the high facade of the castle, the thousand windows. "What if the plan is to blow up this whole building? Make it collapse like those pictures you see of buildings disappearing into their own cloud of debris?"

He didn't answer right away. He watched Margaret Thatcher get into a black car and drive away, like anyone else, a private citizen. So many of the world's celebrities were here, or were on their way here. If Le Tour blew up the castle with everyone in it, what would happen in the world? Movie stars, news anchors, pundits, media moguls, political leaders, the pope, royalty, everyone who was anyone, or had ever been anyone. In the morning they had seen Tammy Faye Bakker without makeup, escorted by two very tall, very imposing boys in Ole Miss jackets. Tammy Faye Bakker. He had turned to Edna and said the name.

"Who's Tammy Faye Bakker?"

"A once-celebrity in the States."

"Oh."

"She was a religious lady who'd paint herself thick as the whore of Babylon and then cry on television so the mascara would run. Teased hair, enough mascara to fertilize a couple of acres of bottomland. She was a sight."

"And you watched her?"

"Sometimes," he said. "For fun. Sure. You don't have religious fakes over here?"

"Not that I've noticed. But then I've been busy."

"My God, *everyone's* here," he said.

A little later, in the enormous, overdone, palatial dining room, he had watched Henry Kissinger and George Shultz come face to face and decide not to speak to each other. Kissinger sat across from Joe

Paterno. John Warner sat at Paterno's side, looking like an undertaker.

Now, parking the little car, with Edna Zuckerman musing in the passenger seat, looking at the castle, he had a moment of foreboding. They were not going to be able to stop Le Tour.

She gathered her coat about her and opened the car door.

How odd, that he could be wondering if she still wanted him, or had been toying with him. How insistent were the demands of simply being alive in the minute, of answering one's desires and wishes, one's need for solace and hopes for comfort. He got out of the car and looked across its wet roof at her. She was not beautiful. This fact rather endeared her to him.

She said, "I guess Thomas will have whatever he's been able to find out."

"It won't be much."

"I guess not—if you say so."

They started away from the car. There were several people standing in a small group near the door. Gorman recognized Brad Pitt, Jane Fonda, Dan Rather, and Tom Brokaw. Brokaw had his hands shoved down into the pockets of his coat and looked uncomfortable. They were all talking to a young man in a ratty leather jacket and jeans, with an angelic face and blond curls, eyes blue as the principle of blue, the *idea* of blue.

"Who is that they're talking to?" Gorman asked as they passed into the cavernous foyer.

"Billy Angel. The new British rock star. He's supposed to be better than Jewel. Well, actually he is. Want to hear one of his lyrics?"

They got to the elevators. He pushed the up button and then hesitated.

"Well?" she said.

He pushed the button again.

"I'm sorry I got so irritable, Ned."

It struck him that she had not spoken his name before. He couldn't remember that she had used the name. He wanted to kiss her.

"I asked if you wanted to hear one of Billy Angel's lyrics."

"Okay," he said.

The elevator opened and Barbara Walters got off, without quite seeing them. They stepped in and the door closed, and now they were looking at a bronze reflection of themselves, wet and still dripping, still shivering. "I wonder what they all thought of us."

"We're security people," she said. "Like Thomas F."

"Oh, Thomas, right."

"Do you want to hear the lyrics?"

He nodded.

She sang, her voice taking on the low whisper of a torch singer, but the melody rambled, and in fact it sounded as though she was making it up as she went along.

It's bad to hate Jews. And not good to be against
　　black people either, or Arabs or
Irish types or Chinese or Japanese too. It's not a good
　　thing.
My mother was codependent and neglected me, and
　　I forgive her

Because I don't hate anyone. I know I can forgive my
   sister too,
Though she got pregnant and didn't know which of
   the football
Guys was the father, and she told Mother I ate all the
   cheese one
Day when I hadn't done any such thing. But that's all
   right because
It's bad to hate, and I try my best not to hate anyone.

She stopped, and looked at him. "That's all I can
remember."

"You're kidding," he said.

"No, I memorized it, because I couldn't believe
people were actually buying it. He's a big star and they
think he's a poet. Especially the teenagers. But I saw
Hugh Downs talking about him as a bloody poet. He's
got a best-selling book of this shit. I wish I was having
you on about it, but it's true and those are the actual
words of the song. It's called 'Me,' by the way. Can you
imagine it? That's where we are. I mean we sort of gave
Shakespeare to the world and we've come so far down,
to this sod with the pretty blue eyes and the blond hair
and the simpering voice."

"Jesus Christ," he said. He had an unbidden moment
of wondering whether it wouldn't be a good thing to let
Le Tour go ahead with his designs on the world of fame
and celebrity, in the name of whatever he cared to
express to the world. He almost said as much to Edna.

They got to her room door. She opened it and they
went inside, and she dropped her coat and flopped

down on the bed, turned on her stomach, and reached for the phone. He stood by the door, still in his coat.

"Should I—" he said.

She held up one hand. Then she spoke into the phone. "Thomas Franklin's room." She waited. He strode to the window and looked out. You could see the golf course—most of the front nine—from this height. There wasn't anyone out there now.

She hung up the phone. "There's no answer."

"We could go down and look for him."

"You get the feeling we shouldn't rest."

He nodded, though his heart sank.

"Did you see *To Catch a Thief* and *The Pink Panther*? All those romantic movies set in expensive places? I saw them all when I was a teenager; I was obsessed with them. We bought all of them on video and I'd watch them over and over."

"Yes?" he said.

"It used to strike me as odd that people could make love and romance each other while their lives were threatened, or bad guys were shooting at them or chasing them. You know?"

"I always thought it was unrealistic."

"Of course," she said. "That's the whole point of it. They aren't supposed to be realistic. If it's realistic Cary Grant falls off the roof. Splat. Dead Cary Grant." She lay over, lazily, on her back. "Sometimes I wonder if Americans have the subtlety necessary for romance."

"Probably not," he said.

"You want to go downstairs."

"No," he said.

Rita undressed and crossed the room to the wet bar and poured herself a tall glass of malt scotch. Not her drink, but then she was loading up for Alfonzo. Outside the window it was raining. A downpour that had started as mist. On the sofa in the sitting room part of her suite was Thomas Franklin, holding his own drink, a glass of tonic water, which he drank nervously, watching her come back to his part of the room. She sat down in the chair at his left and sipped the whiskey. It went down smoothly.

"So—" Franklin said. "You took the ball out of your bag. Was the bag ever out of your hands?"

"Of course it was, honey. You don't think I'd carry that thing with me, do you?" She crossed her legs. There was a perverse kind of joy in making men she had no designs on feel as though she had such designs. She liked to do it to nice men who would not cross the line and whose fright gave her a strange thrill. Of course, in a way, this was what had happened with Alfonzo the first time, and it had gotten out of hand. Well, she had been drinking. Lots of things happened when she had been tooting up, or drinking. She sipped the whiskey and leaned slightly toward Franklin, smiling, while he tried to think of the next question. The poor castle security man, the Castle Man, she had called him. She looked at the odd way his eyes were, the unevenness of them. She thought of *The Hunchback of Notre Dame*.

She'd never seen it and supposed it was a football movie.

"Can you not think of how or when someone would have put an explosive in one of your golf balls?"

"Somebody could have slipped it to me anywhere. They make them in the novelty shops."

"Exploding golf balls."

"I already told you this," she said. "Sprague told you this. Alfonzo told you this."

"I just—you see, there's a situation—well, never mind."

"You can tell me," she said.

"No, I—listen. Who has—if you can give me the names of whoever has or had access to your golf bag."

"Well, no." She leaned even closer. "*Lots* of people had access." She paused for effect. "To my golf bags."

"I see." He swallowed.

"Are you sure you don't want something a little stronger?"

"I can't," he said.

He wasn't such a bad-looking man, really. The eyes were actually kind of interesting. His nervousness made him almost cute. He stood and sighed and seemed discouraged. "We'll have to examine yer other golf balls."

"You want to look at my balls?" she said.

"I'm afraid we'll have to check them."

Such a funny way of talking. "You want to check my balls."

He seemed to be walking in place. "If you don't mind."

She said, "I don't have any more than the ones that were in my bag, and you already looked at those."

"Yes," he said. He excused himself and moved to the door.

"Anything else?" she said.

He paused and seemed confused. "I'll—I'll let you know."

"Bye," she said.

He went out with an alacrity that was like flight. One thing she had learned about men was that they seemed to lose intelligence in direct proportion to how aroused they were. There were all the jokes about it, of course, but she had concrete proof that the jokes were only slight exaggerations. You could not get a thought from a man while he was in that state; whereas she could wander the world of thought and ideas while fucking. It had nothing to do with her sometimes. It was a form of relaxation or it was a working out of frustration or it was a rage or a tantrum or an attack—or simply an aspect of an old habit, routine as eating. A little hunger, a little itch. She was tremendously good at golf when she was right, when she was on, and the world had laid things at her feet as a result of this. She had taken what she wanted, and it seemed that she always wanted more. And if sometimes she lay awake in the dark and felt the terrors of having gone so far over the line of the rest of practical society and social law, she awakened each morning with a fresh hunger, and a fresh sense that she would find a way to make it all come out right. It wouldn't be reform, quite. She would be a woman of experience, who had come to a sort of plateau. She liked to imagine herself like Kate Hepburn, having reached this stage after a lifetime of doing exactly as she wished. What puzzled her was the price—the price of the last few years had been so heavy. She wondered how others managed it without falling into the consequences so heavily. Her drug use was not anything but a way of trying to keep the consequences of the other thing at bay, the sense that she had been such a bad girl, a girl who would break Daddy's heart, as she had in fact done. She had, as a matter of astringent fact, seduced her own father out of a wish to get back at her mother for being strict with her. Well, she hadn't actually seduced him. She had made him nervous. She had caused him to leave the house, and her mother had never guessed at any of it. Her mother thought he was going through male menopause. He was terrified. And now he lived in Spain and went to bullfights and had grown a beard, a gray beard like Hemingway's had been, and he was writing bad fiction and calling younger women "daughter." Rita addressed her letters to him as "Papa." It would be funny if it weren't so sad.

He sent her his stories. Stories with opening lines like: "Jim Weatherby's hands were big and red and hairy as lobsters." Or, "The woman danced across the floor, her legs screaming."

Bad, bad.

Poor man. She had ruined a perfectly nice CEO. She thought of him, swallowing the whiskey. Alfonzo would be at the door soon enough, planning a week's stay. Alfonzo was part of the price. She wished for some clarity, and had more of the whiskey. It never quite provided any clarity, but it made the wish for it dissolve. Nothing was working. She went into the bathroom and looked at herself. Billy Sprague had been nice. She had felt something with him, a little something. There had been a desperation about him. After the putt, and the exploding ball, he seemed changed, if she could be assumed to have known him well enough to notice a change. His attitude about the bet with Alfonzo, and her part in it, was nearly cavalier. It was as if the whole thing no longer mattered.

She brushed her hair with her fingers, looked into her own mouth. She cleaned her teeth, then went with her whiskey back into the living room. She turned on the television. Movies, movies, sitcoms, CNN. The news-people were strangers, faces she didn't recognize—how odd to realize that the important ones were all here, in these posh rooms. And in the rooms of all the hotels in the surrounding towns.

The knock at the door did not surprise her.

She poured more of the whiskey, then thought better of it and went to her purse for some Valium. She took that, then swallowed more whiskey. The knocking sounded, peremptory, louder than before.

She looked through the peephole. Sprague. Quickly she opened the door and pulled him in, then looked out, up and down the long corridor with its fake gas lamps going on as far as she could see. She stepped in and closed the door. Sprague was standing with his back to her across the room, looking out the window.

"The putt would've gone in," he said.

She said, "Yes."

"Son of a bitch if it wouldn't."

"It was dead solid perfect," she said.

He turned. "I feel good."

"Want a drink?" she said.

"No."

"I'm glad you feel good."

He stood there gazing at her, rocking back and forth on the balls of his feet.

"So," she said.

"So we have to make Alfonzo admit that."

She drank. "Good luck." Her head spun and made her have to look for the chair. She found it in the sudden swirl and sat down. She remembered when this same sudden sense of disequilibrium had caused her to falter backward and then tumble down the bank and into the water surrounding the seventeenth green at Sawgrass, in front of a national audience. She held both arms of the chair and tried to fix her eyes on Sprague, who had divided and become liquid.

"I'm here to convince him," Sprague said out of the blur he had become.

"You're nice."

"I love you, Rita."

"Gawd," she said. She tried to stand but couldn't. She did not want any talk of love. Not now. Maybe not ever. Sprague had interested her — still did — but she wanted no talk of any love, or any of that endearment stuff, the small talk of married couples. It appalled her. It was something to run from. "Go," she said. Or thought she said.

He had come to her side. He actually knelt there and took her hand. "Rita, I want to marry you. Let's play this one round of golf and then go somewhere far away and start over."

She was completely speechless. She seemed to look through a long tunnel at his face, his earnest, newly confident face. "You would've sunk a fucking putt," she tried to say. "And that's changed your life?" She couldn't get it out.

"Rita, tell me you'll marry me."

"You know what would be fun?" she said. "It'd be fun if the whole fucking world blew up. Not jus' a fucking golf ball but the whole goddamn thing. Boom. All of us trailing off into space. Think of it." Had she said any of this? He still held her hand. He had taken both her hands, and she had no recollection of when he had done it.

"Rita?" he said.

"What." He had heard that. She said it again. "What?"

"Are you all right?"

"I'm fucked."

"No," he said. "We're gonna fix it. Alfonzo has to admit that ball was going in. Rita, for the first time in my life I feel really free. I can't explain it. I feel like I can breathe out—for the first time in my life, Rita. And it's this—this feeling I have for you. I love you."

She said, or tried to say, "I've fucked enough different men to people a small country." It wouldn't come out. He kissed her hands, then leaned over her knees to kiss her cheek. "Hey," she said. "Lighten up." None of it quite got out. He kissed her mouth now, pulled her up out of the chair, and then lay her down on the floor. He was kissing her mouth, and something else was happening. She closed her eyes and then opened them again. The kissing went on, and she realized with a start that he was blowing into her mouth, frantically administering mouth-to-mouth resuscitation. That was what it was. She had tried to reach down to take hold of his

160

prick, and he was saving her life. Or he thought he was saving her life.

"You stopped breathing," he said. "You were gone."

"I was not. Will you let me get up?"

"Darling, I'm sure you'd stopped breathing."

He pulled her to a sitting position, then to her feet. He had his hands under her arms, and it tickled. "Stop it," she said.

"I thought you were dying," he said. "I asked you to marry me and you stopped breathing."

"Okay," she said.

"You'll marry me?" he said.

"Whatever you say."

"I love you."

"Right."

"Do you love me?"

"Jesus. I'm dizzy," she said. "I can't stand up."

"Darling," he said. "What've you taken?"

"Taken a lot of shit," she said. "Almost fucked the castle guy."

"I can't understand what you're saying," Sprague told her.

"Castle security guy was a citizen."

"Yes? The answer *is* yes, right?—you'll marry me."

"You're a citizen."

"What?"

"Bed," she got out.

He moved with her into the bedroom, and she lay down in the spinning of the room. Sprague was there, going by and going by. It was as if she were on a train platform, watching eleven Spragues go by one after the other after the other.

"Can I stay with you?" he said.

She could see how gallant he felt. They were all so pathetic when they were gallant, all wound up trying to get into position to use their little tallywackers. Who was it who had called it his tallywacker? She couldn't remember. Someone she didn't like very much had called it his tallywacker. Somebody else had called it his mashie. Another had said it was his driver. Christ, she was sick of all of them. The only true feeling was standing there watching the little ball disappear into the distance, getting smaller and smaller, flying, landing so slow so far away. Go away, she wanted to say, but he sat down at her side and was resting one hand on her hip. That felt good; it was tactile. His hand was warm. She looked at the back of it, and then she touched it, almost curious.

"Oh, my love," Billy Sprague said.

In another room on the same floor of the castle, Ned Gorman and Edna Zuckerman lay quiet, listening to the rain on the windows. Thomas Franklin had called the room, and Edna had answered. She had told him she was going to sleep for an hour. She had said she didn't know where Ned Gorman was; she hadn't seen him since they came back from the ride up into the bluffs surrounding the castle. She didn't think the exploding golf ball was connected to Le Tour, or the missing plastique, and people had to rest. Every now and then people had to lie down and go to sleep.

As she spoke in this manner to Franklin, Gorman thought about the strangeness of what she was saying — even in war, in battles, ongoing conflicts, people had to lie down, and be unconscious for hours at a time. Le Tour would have to rest too. The implacable enemy would have to spend hours in a state of perfect helplessness. Edna Zuckerman hung up the phone and lay back down, and for a long interval neither of them had spoken.

"You were involved once," Gorman said. "Right?"

She sighed. "Once."

"Married?"

She sighed again. "No."

"But intimate."

"Jesus."

"I'm sorry. It's none of my business, I guess."

"You think this is recreational."

"Pardon me?"

She leaned up on one elbow. "You think this is casual?"

He couldn't find anything to say.

"Oh," she said. "I get it. It's casual for *you*."

"No," he said.

"I've wanted you for real ever since the train platform, and I think Thomas knows it, too."

"Is Thomas likely to get jealous?"

She lay back. "Yes."

After a pause, he said, "And what form is his jealousy likely to take?"

"Oh," she said. "A rather violent form."

He sat up. "As in?"

"When we were together and I was teaching—I had this job teaching, as undercover—we were trying to catch a professor of engineering who had secrets and who we thought was selling them to the highest bidder. Anyway, the professor turned out to be innocent and kind of charming, and I had this fling. Nothing serious. We didn't even sleep together. We had a couple of romantic dinners on the sly and tried to decide if we wanted to. You see, he was married and rather honorable and all that, and so was I. But we were drawn to each other, and so we met those two times, and—well, Thomas found out about it, and he went over to the professor's house and bashed in the door and just generally knocked him about a bit, you know, for an hour or two."

"An *hour* or *two*."

"Something close to it."

"He doesn't look like he could do a thing like that."

"Oh, he can."

"I mean he doesn't look like he's strong enough."

"Well, he had help."

"He had . . ."

She nodded. "A seven-iron, I believe it was."

Gorman lay there with an ache deep in his stomach, thinking about an hour or two with a man wielding a seven-iron.

"Now you know why I hate golf."

"Wait a minute . . . He wouldn't . . ."

"Do you have any fags?" she asked. "I could use a smoke. I mean I quit smoking a year ago and still when I get nervous I want a smoke, and I usually carry them

164

for that reason and just now I feel like a smoke and I'm out."

"What would he do if he knew we . . ." Gorman couldn't say the words.

"I don't know. That was two years ago with the professor."

"Jesus Christ, and they put you on assignment together?"

"We were partners before any of this got started. I mean, how do you think any of it got started? We got very good at hiding it, of course. In fact it got to be a habit. It might even be what eventually broke us up."

"Well, I'll be goddamned."

They were quiet.

She said, "I wish I had a cigarette."

"I wish you'd told me some of this before we —" He halted.

"What would you have done?"

"I don't know. I don't know but I would like not to be humping somebody whose ex-boyfriend uses golf clubs on people, that's all. I mean I just would like it better if no ex-boyfriend or golf club entered into it. It strikes me that that would be a good thing. That would be something to aim at."

"If he had his way, I'd never sleep with anyone."

"You mean he's still . . ."

"He doesn't know," she said. "I don't see why you're so worried."

Gorman got out of the bed and reached for his clothes. He had never felt so naked in his life. He couldn't get them on fast enough.

"What're you doing?" she said.

"I'm getting the hell out of here."

"You're being ridiculous."

"Yeah. Well, remember—we never did this. I want to get back to my room in case Thomas calls or comes by. There's only so many places a person can be here."

"It's a big castle. He's probably in his own room, sleeping. People have to sleep."

"I sleep heavy. Tell him that I sleep heavy. I don't hear somebody knocking on my door. No, you don't tell him that. I'll tell him that. Jesus Christ, how could you do this to me?"

"I haven't done anything to you. You're overreacting. It's bloody stupid."

"Yeah," he said. "And you hate golf."

"Don't leave," she said. "Please?"

"I just hope it's not too late."

"I'll tell him we did this if you leave."

He stood there, half in, half out of his pants. "Edna, you're—this is a joke. It's—you're joking with me."

"I'm serious. I'll tell him."

"No, I mean about the whole thing—the whole golf club story and the professor and all that."

"The professor had his arms and legs broken. Both arms, both legs. They weren't compound fractures. But they were broken. He had to dial the phone with his nose to call the police. But then he didn't, finally, decide to press charges."

"What is this?" Gorman said. "That's simple assault. The police can press charges."

"Well, no complaint was filed."

He went to the door and looked out the peephole. The corridor looked empty.

"I'm telling you," Edna said. "I don't want you to leave."

"Okay," he said, coming back. "How long do you want me to stay?"

She moved one leg. "Long enough."

"Edna, couldn't we meet again at a later time, say when Thomas isn't along?"

"I like the danger."

"Danger—for you? What danger—that you'll be sickened by the sound of my breaking bones? We've got a mad bomber to catch, and I know that people have to lie down and rest now and then and all that, but we had fifteen good minutes here and I think that's enough rest. I think that's more than enough rest, at least for me, Edna, *please* don't make me stay any longer. Because what if I'm lying in a hospital miles from here and we still haven't found the plastique?"

She had come from under the blankets and was on all fours, moving to the edge of the bed and licking her lips. Her features were ugly in the lascivious leer she affected, and he wondered how he had missed this ugliness a few moments earlier, wondered how he could have been stupid enough to miss the real relation between her and Franklin.

"You want to find the plastique," he said feebly. "Don't you?"

Rita got out of bed and went to the window. The rain was still coming down, but softer now. She could see a small break in the grayness far out toward the sea, a little shaft of something like sunlight. She opened the sash and leaned out. There was a ledge. She was very weirdly drunk—drunk with a kind of acumen, a sharpening of everything. She had ingested a little cocaine. She had swallowed some Benzedrine. One pill. A pick-me-up. Sprague was asleep on the bed. He looked guilty lying there. It was in the way his legs were curled up, his hands covering his face. Whoever said sleep was innocent? She climbed out on the ledge. What he would say when he woke and found her out here, where it was high and wet and far. She had no plans of dropping or falling or jumping. She knew this was dangerous and wanted to experience it. Everything had always been about her craving for more experience. There was never enough. She stood out on the ledge and moved from her window to the next one. The ledge was plenty wide enough—it felt sheer and dangerous because there was no railing, of course; but the ledge was a good three feet wide. Lots of room. She slid along with her back to the window, then she turned, carefully, so she could look in the next one. The bricks of the castle were uneven, so there were even places to hold on. She took herself to the next window, looked in. Empty rooms. She moved along, and here, in his bed with his pants down around his knees, was Castle Man, Mr. Franklin. She knew Mr. Franklin was dreaming about her. It was flattering, almost sweet. She moved one more window over, another empty room, so she went back to Mr. Franklin's again. She told herself she wanted to see the finale. But

Mr. Franklin seemed to be having some trouble bringing things to a conclusion. It came to her with a pang that, in his imagination, she was not cooperating very well. There was a look of frustrated anger on his face. He was concentrating, eyes closed. It struck her that here she was, naked, the goddess of his dreams, balanced on the ledge, on the sky right outside, so near, and she could give him the thrill of his life.

So she knocked on the window.

He opened his eyes, then seemed to gather his whole body in a bunch there in the middle of the bed. He rolled over — she saw his ass; it looked purple for some reason — and then he was standing, pulling the pants up. She tried to signal him, wanting him to know it was all right for him to continue. She wanted to say how flattered she was. But then he looked angry, outraged, and she decided to move along the ledge, past the next empty room and the next. She went on, moving with some speed. The air was cold now, and she was beginning to feel that this experience hadn't been all that glorious. But she was curious as to what she would find in the next window, and then the next, on to the end of the long, massive wall. She got about eleven rooms down from her own when another sash opened and someone — it was Franklin, she knew — leaned out.

"You!" he said.

She waved at him. "Hi."

"You—" He stopped. "Don't do it!" This was said only halfheartedly.

"I would've stood there so you could finish," she said.

He leaned farther out. "What?"

And now, eleven windows back down the ledge,

Sprague leaned out to call along the windswept height. "Good God, Rita!" he yelled. "Not now! Not after what we've decided!"

She said, "Billy, meet Mr. Franklin."

"I met Mr. Franklin," he called. Mr. Franklin had nodded embarrassedly to Billy, then looked back at her.

"Mr. Franklin was dreaming of me, weren't you, Mr. Franklin?"

"This is most irregular," Mr. Franklin said. "I shall call the police."

"I thought you were the police."

"Rita," Sprague called. "I'm coming out."

"You stay there," she called back to him. "Don't you dare or I swear I *will* jump!"

"Rita, you don't have to sleep with him. I promise."

She moved to the next window, and here she saw a man and a woman, both naked, the man sitting on the bed and the woman lying back with one leg bent at the knee. She looked languid and happy, and the man looked quite miserable.

"Rita, please!"

She tapped on the window. It seemed perfectly natural—naked people, naked together, separated only by a little matter of a window. They looked frightened. Especially, Rita thought, the man. The man looked abject. He didn't come to the window, as Rita thought he might. He jumped and then he dove behind the bed. The woman rose and walked over though. Rita moved back along the wall so she could open the sash.

"Hi," she said.

The woman said, "Yes. Fourteen floors, I think."

"No," Rita said. "I meant 'Hi' as in hello."

"Oh. Hello."

Rita indicated Mr. Franklin. "Meet my friend, Mr. Franklin."

Mr. Franklin yelled, "I had not a thing to do with her, Edna."

"Mr. Franklin was dreaming about me. I saw him. Imagine the treat. You actually see a man fantasizing about you. And there you are, standing in the sky."

"I never!" screamed Mr. Franklin.

All through this, Sprague was calling to her. "Rita! Oh, no—Rita, *please*."

"Perhaps you should go back inside," the woman said. It dawned on Rita that she did not like the name Edna. She had played against someone named Edna years ago in a pro-am, and she had beat the pants off her. And that Edna had proved a rather bad sport, saying to the cameras that she was off her game or she would've won. Rita had said to the same cameras, "Look, none of us is playing each other. We're all playing the course."

This seemed like the thing to say now. So she looked at Edna and said exactly that.

Edna spoke past her. "You just wait, Thomas. Two can play this game. You know who I've got in here with me?"

The man who was in the room with Edna shouted, "I JUST STOPPED BY TO TALK ABOUT THE BOMB!" He got a shirt on so quickly, but he was still naked from the waist down. "REALLY, THOMAS. I JUST THIS MINUTE STOPPED BY!"

Rita pointed at him below the waist. "Uh, Mr. Franklin, I think he's been here awhile."

Sprague was calling her name.

"Let's all get out on the ledge without our clothes," Rita said. It seemed like a great idea. She felt the cold on her skin like a caress. She could see that Sprague had no shirt and remembered that he was naked too. It was wonderful. It seemed like the finest idea.

Mr. Franklin was talking to Edna and the other man. "Okay. I think I have it parsed, I think I have it bloody well figured out."

"You have it figured out," Edna said. "And I've got you and this tart figured out."

"My name is Rita, thank you."

"She came from over there," Mr. Franklin screamed. "And now you've done it, Edna. You've gone over the line again."

"I WAS JUST HERE LOOKING FOR THE BOMB!" the other man yelled.

"A bomb?" Rita said. "Who's talking about a bomb? What bomb?"

Mr. Franklin had ducked back into his room.

"Oh, Jesus Christ," the other man said and began running around, picking up his clothes. "How the hell are we supposed to work together if he's breaking my arms and legs, for Christ's sake."

"I hope I haven't caused any trouble," Rita said to Edna, who closed the window in her face. Now there was just poor Sprague, leaning out with that pleading look on his face. "All I need is a horse and some long hair," Rita said to him.

"Please," he said. "Please come back."

"Okay," Rita said.

It was easy. The ledge was wet, it was still raining a little, and she moved with sure feet and wide strides to her window and in. Sprague grabbed her as she crossed the sill of the window and held tight to her, and she realized that she was quite cold. She couldn't stop shivering. There was a commotion out in the corridor, banging, shouts. She was warm; Sprague had covered her with the blankets from the bed, and being so warm after the cold, she was abruptly very sleepy. So sleepy. She let him hold her, poor, silly Billy Sprague, whose life had turned around on a putt that exploded, like a little bomb, and as she drifted off into a rare, peaceful sleep, she wondered if this weren't the bomb that unfortunate man had been yelling about.

Chapter Seven

FREE DROP

by Dave Barry

"She was *naked*," said Sheena Cameron, crouched in the underbrush where she and François Le Tour had set up their observation post.

"Oh yes," said Le Tour. "Very." He was still looking through his binoculars toward the castle ledge from which Rita had just disappeared.

"What the hell was she *doing* out there?" asked Sheena.

"I have no idea," said Le Tour, still looking.

"Well," said Sheena, "she's gone now."

"Yes," said Le Tour, a bit too regretfully for Sheena's liking.

"So why are you still looking?" she asked.

"She might come back," said Le Tour, a bit too hopefully for Sheena's liking.

"She's a big one, isn't she?" she said. "Bit of an Amazon?"

"Yes," said Le Tour, thinking about the jiggle of Rita's breasts, the way her thigh muscles rippled when she moved. He was imagining what it would be like to be in the grip of those legs.

"A woman like that, she gets a little older, she puts on the pounds," said Sheena. "In a few years, she's a cow."

"Yes," said Le Tour, still looking at the ledge.

"A great fat lactating cow," said Sheena.

"Yes," said Le Tour.

"Moo," said Sheena.

"Yes," said Le Tour.

"You're not listening to me," said Sheena.

"Yes," said Le Tour.

Sheena yanked the binoculars away, startling Le Tour.

"What?" he said, turning to her.

"We're supposed to be overthrowing the old world order," she said. "And you're waiting for the return of Miss Tits on a Tightrope."

Le Tour smiled. He liked it when he made women jealous. And he had found that he could make any woman jealous.

"Miss Shaughnessy has excellent balance," he said.

"Oh, it's her *balance* you were admiring," said Sheena, pissed off because she considered herself the kind of woman who *never* got jealous. "Perhaps you'd like her to balance on your pole."

"Perhaps," said Le Tour, pondering it, which made Sheena even angrier. "But first, as you say, we have work to do."

"Aye," said Angus MacLout, who along with Ox Ferguson had crept up to join them. Both men were filthy, their faces streaked with mud. "We're finished out there." He pointed with the shovel he held out toward the manicured links. "Time to show Phillip Bates who the true master of Rathgarve is. Time to end two hundred years of injustice. Time to return Angus MacLout to his rightful place."

Le Tour glanced at Sheena. "He says it's time."

"Indeed it is," Sheena said. She reached into her handbag and withdrew a pistol.

"What's that?" Angus said.

Ox grunted.

Sheena fired and there came a chuffing sound. A black dot appeared in the middle of Angus's broad forehead. He wavered a moment, then pitched over backward.

Ox had not moved. The look he gave Sheena suggested that he had expected as much all along. There was a second muffled report from Sheena's silenced pistol and Ox toppled over Angus with a sigh that sounded very much like a grunt.

"I believe Angus has assumed his rightful place," Le Tour observed.

"Thoughtful of him to bring a shovel," Sheena said, replacing the pistol in her bag.

"Wasn't it?" Le Tour asked.

"Before we get to that," said Sheena, as blithely as if she'd just rung off on a troublesome phone call, "I want to talk about this plan of yours."

"What about it?" asked Le Tour.

"Well it's fucked now, isn't it?" she said.

"What do you mean?"

"I mean, in case your memory stopped working because all your blood rushed to your other head, Miss Naked over there had her golf ball blow up on the golf course today."

Le Tour, looking irritatingly amused, said, "So?"

"So the place is already crawling with security, and now they're on to us," said Sheena. "They'll check every golf ball ten times before they let it get near the big shots. I can't *believe* you left that ball in her bag. What a *stupid* fucking mistake."

Le Tour was still smiling. "Did it not occur to you," he said, "that perhaps it was not a mistake?"

"*What?*" said Sheena.

"I left the ball in her bag on purpose," said Le Tour. "And it blew up right when I wanted it to."

"Why?"

"Because now the fools will be looking for exploding balls," said Le Tour. He used the toe of his shoe to lift Angus's chin a few inches off the damp ground, then let it drop again.

He prodded Ox but got no grunt. Satisfied, he glanced up at Sheena. "Which is exactly what I want them to do."

"This is fucking *crazy*," Ned Gorman was saying, more to himself than to Edna. He slammed the window closed and began pulling on his pants. "I can't fucking *believe* I did this."

"What's the rush?" asked Edna.

"What's the rush?" Gorman asked, his voice breaking. "What's the fucking *rush*? We have the most powerful people in the world in this castle right now, and we have François fucking Le Tour, a world-class terrorist, running around with enough plastique to blow this whole place to hell. And *now* I find out that your fucking boyfriend is—"

"*Former* fucking boyfriend," interrupted Edna.

"Excuse me, your *former* fucking boyfriend is a wacko psycho who any minute now is going to be pounding on the—"

Someone pounded on the door.

"Open the door, dammit!" It was indeed Franklin.

"Shit," said Ned. He went quickly to the window and looked at the ledge, pondering an escape. But it was a long, sickening way to the ground, and Ned was not big on heights.

"Calm down," said Edna.

"Calm *down*?" said Ned. "Calm DOWN?"

"OPEN THE FUCKING DOOR!" shouted Franklin. "I'M NOT GOING TO HURT YOU."

Ned warily approached the door. "You're not?" he asked.

"We don't have time to fight over that whore," said Franklin.

"WHO ARE YOU CALLING A WHORE?" shouted Edna, striding to the door and yanking it open to reveal Franklin and, walking past in the hallway, Alan Greenspan, who nodded politely but did not in any way appear to register the fact that Edna was stark naked.

"I'm calling *you* a whore, you whore," said Franklin.

"And what about your naked golf lady?" sneered Edna. "Was she showing you how to grip your putter?"

"I didn't touch her!" said Franklin. "She showed up in my fucking window!"

"Oh, *right*," said Edna. "You expect me to believe— Oh, hello, sir!" She gave a little friendly wave to Prince Charles, who was walking past with two bodyguards and trying, with zero success, not to notice Edna's body.

"Let's get out of the hall," said Ned, drawing Franklin into the room and closing the door. "Listen," he said to Franklin. "We're supposed to be professionals. We need to set aside our personal business here and get to work."

"Agreed," said Franklin.

"Okay," said Ned, much relieved that Franklin was over his jealousy. "Now where do we stand?"

"We've doubled the security at the estate perimeter," said Franklin, whose plan was to kill Ned later. "We've added another perimeter outside of that, with constant patrols in the buffer zone between the two. We have two AWACS planes doing surveillance of the airspace in twelve-hour rotations, and have fighters in the air 'round the clock. Nobody, *nobody* can get in or out of here without our knowing it."

"It's who's already here that I'm worried about," said Ned.

"Aye, that's our big problem now," said Franklin. "That, and the fucking Semtex."

"That's what it is?" asked Edna. "You're sure?"

"Aye," said Franklin, not looking at her, still talking to Ned. "We don't have the final results yet, but looks like the golf ball that blew up was from the batch we've been looking for. Looks like our boy Le Tour smuggled the plastique in that way—he just fucked up and left one ball in the lady's bag."

"Lady?" sniffed Edna.

"Whatever," said Franklin. "Point is, Le Tour's got enough of that shit left to turn this whole fucking castle into a crater. He's on the grounds somewhere, and we've got to find him."

"And now he knows we're on to him," said Ned.

"Maybe not," said Franklin. "We've put out the story that we think the exploding ball was just a prank. So far, people seem to be buying it. Somebody inside this castle has to be working with that fucker Le Tour. We're hoping our story gets to him. We're hoping he lets his guard down."

"Let's hope," said Ned. "Meanwhile, what's our plan?"

"First thing," said Franklin, "we search every fucking room in this place. Bates is throwing his big welcome banquet tonight; all the guests are heading there now. While they eat, we go room to room till we find the Semtex."

"And if we don't find it?" asked Ned.

"Then at least we know the castle is safe," said Franklin. "We work the grounds next."

"Do we have explosive-sniffing dogs?"

"They should be arriving downstairs"—Franklin checked his watch— "right about now."

"Let's go," said Ned, turning toward the door, glad to be back at work.

"Right," said Franklin, following.

"I'll catch up," said the still-naked Edna. "Let me just throw some clothes on."

Neither man answered. The door slammed shut,

leaving Edna alone. She moved to the door and listened for a moment, then walked over to a floor lamp standing near the window. She unscrewed the fastener holding the lampshade on, then removed the lampshade and set it down, exposing the bulb. She moved the lamp so that it was right next to the window, then turned it on. The bulb's harsh light illuminated her body. Grunting, Edna raised the window and leaned out, feeling the cold rain on her breasts. She stood still for a moment, staring into the distance. Then she slowly raised her right hand and held it in front of her, using her thumb and forefinger to make the "okay" sign. She held it for a full ten seconds.

Out on the rainswept bluff, peering through his binoculars, Le Tour saw the sign and smiled.

"Ain't we going to the banquet?" asked Jake Turmoil.

"Not straightaway we're not," answered Billy Angel. "Not till I get my head right."

"I got nothin' with me," said Jake Turmoil, whose real name was Nigel Frimpett. He had been required to change it when he was hired as the head bodyguard to Billy Angel, whose real name was Harry Pudd. "You told me to leave the bleedin' briefcase in London."

The briefcase contained enough high-grade cocaine to severely impair both houses of Parliament. Usually it was in the possession of a trusted member of the Billy Angel entourage, who was under strict orders never to be more than a few steps away from Billy Angel. It was a system patterned after the one used to make sure the president of the United States always had access to the nuclear launch codes, except that Billy Angel used his access a lot more often than the president used his.

"I *know* we haven't got the bleedin' briefcase," said Billy Angel. "I met somebody who's gonna help us out."

"Who?" asked Jake Turmoil.

"Woman," said Billy Angel, who was used to being offered things by women. "We're to meet her on the golf course, fourth tee, in ten minutes' time."

"Christ, you sure?" asked Jake Turmoil. "There's bleedin' cops every—"

"I *know* there's bleedin' cops every bleedin' where," said Billy Angel. "That's why were goin' out in the bleedin' *rain*. But I am fucked if I'm gonna go sit in that bleedin' banquet next to Al bleedin' Gore and listen to him babble about global bleedin' warmin' without first takin' somethin' for my bleedin' head."

"Al Gore?" said Jake Turmoil, who did not follow current events. "The football player?"

"Bleedin' Christ," said Billy Angel, heading out the main castle door into the rain.

The rain was starting to drive Sheena crazy, dripping from her hair into her eyes, slowly soaking through her allegedly waterproof jacket and hood. The cold was also getting to her, especially her feet, which she knew were going to hurt like hell when they regained feeling, if they ever did.

But what was *really* pissing her off was Le Tour, who for nearly thirty minutes had just stood there, smiling smugly, like a man enjoying a day at the beach. He had made it clear he wanted her to be quiet, but she couldn't stand it anymore.

"Will you please tell me what the *fuck* is going on?" she hissed.

"Not now," he said.

"Yes," she said. "*Now.* I have killed people for you, and I have let you screw me, and now I am out here getting pneumonia because of you, and I want to know *what is going on.*"

Le Tour sighed. "What do you want to know?"

"For one thing, I want to know why you let that golf ball explode."

"I told you. So that the fools would look for exploding golf balls."

"Yes, but *why*? Do you want them to find the Semtex? Why did we go to all that trouble to *bring* it here if we aren't going to *use* it?"

"But we *are* using it."

"I don't understand. I thought we were going to blow this place up, with all those people in it. Isn't that the whole fucking *point*? How do we do that if they find the Semtex?"

Le Tour shook his head, a teacher disappointed with his pupil.

"Sheena," he said. "Think for a moment. Suppose we did that. Suppose we blew this castle up, killed all the heads of state, the pope, the media, everybody. Then what?"

"Well, then, there would be, I guess . . . I mean there would be chaos," said Sheena. "Worldwide economic collapse. Anarchy. Right?"

Le Tour gave her a pitying look.

"Sheena," he said, "you are a smart woman, and you are wonderful in the bed. But you are also *very* naive."

"What do you mean?" asked Sheena, wanting to hate him for calling her naive, but undeniably flattered by what he'd said about her in bed.

"I mean," he said, "if we blow up this castle, if we kill all these so-called world leaders, *nothing* will happen. These people are *figureheads*. If we kill them, the world will be shocked, yes—everybody will say a terrible thing happened here, a tragedy. There will be many big, sad televised funerals. And before the coffins are in the ground, there will be new figureheads, no different from the ones we killed. Oh, they will make some noise, declare war on terrorism, but otherwise things will go on exactly as before. Because the institutions that these fig-ureheads *think* they lead—the governments, the armies, the multinational corporations—have far too much invested in the way the world works now to let it be changed just because we kill these preening, self-important people who think they rule the world—these fools who came here, lured by their own vanity, to play a stupid *game*."

Sheena stared into the gloom, rain dripping into her eyes, trying to comprehend what she was hearing. Softly she said, "So we're *not* going to blow them up?"

"Maybe a few," said Le Tour, "to reinforce the Semtex diversion. But no, that is not our plan."

"Then . . . what *is* our plan?"

Le Tour looked at her for a few moments, as if deciding whether or not to trust her. Finally he said, "Think of a computer virus."

"What?"

"A computer virus," he repeated. "What does it do?"

"It . . . it causes the computer to malfunction."

"Yes, but in a certain way. It does not *destroy* the computer. It takes over the computer. It infects it. It *uses* it."

Sheena was frowning at him, trying to see where he was going.

"And if it is a particularly well-designed virus," said Le Tour, "it uses the host computer to connect with, and transmit itself to, another computer, which in turn connects with—"

"I got that," said Sheena impatiently. "I know how a computer virus works. What does that have to do with this golf tournament?"

Le Tour smiled indulgently. "Imagine," he said, "if you had devised a wonderfully sophisticated computer virus. If you wanted to do maximum damage with it, what computers would you want to infect? Would you want to infect little home PCs where children play video games?"

"No," said Sheena, thinking about it. "I'd want to infect the biggest, most powerful . . . *wait a minute.* We're not really talking about computers, are we?"

"No," said Le Tour.

"We're taking about a virus that infects *people.*"

Le Tour's smiled broadened. He was proud of his pupil now. "Go on," he said.

"You're talking about something . . . something like a virus . . . that will infect the world leaders here . . . something that will control their behavior, and . . ."

"Yes?" encouraged Le Tour.

". . . something that *they can pass on to others*, after they leave," Sheena said.

"Very good!" said Le Tour.

"My God," said Sheena, thinking about it. "If you could control *these* people, and they passed the virus along to the people under them, and *they* passed it along to the people under *them*, in no time you'd control . . ."

"Yes?"

". . . my God," said Sheena, "you'd control *the whole fucking world*."

Le Tour's smile was radiant now.

"But how does it—"

"Ssssh," hissed Le Tour, cutting her off. "They're coming."

"I don't see nobody," said Jake Turmoil, peering through the rain.

"She said she'd be here," said Billy Angel, jumping up and down to keep warm. "Fourth tee. That bitch better not be . . . Oh, here she is. Hello, luv."

"Hello, Billy," said the petite woman approaching

them. She'd obviously been waiting in the rain for quite a while. Her hooded jacket was soaked.

"So where is it?" asked Billy Angel.

"That's it?" asked the woman. "Just, where is it? No more sweet talk? I thought we were gonna get together, Billy. I thought you thought I was cute."

"Listen," said Billy Angel, "I'm bleedin' freezin' out here and I haven't got time for this shit. Just give it to me, okay?"

Jake Turmoil stepped forward in a threatening manner, which, as Billy Angel's bodyguard, was mainly what he did. "He says give it to him, bitch," he said.

"Okay, Billy," said Sheena. "I'll give it to you."

It took her just a hair over one second to break Billy Angel's neck and another two to break Jake Turmoil's. Usually she'd have been quicker, but her hands were almost numb.

"Who's the big one?" asked Le Tour, sauntering up.

"Bodyguard," said Sheena.

"Ah," said Le Tour. "Can't be too careful."

It took them ten minutes to strip the bodies and bury them in a sand trap. In another two minutes, Le Tour had changed into Billy Angel's ratty leather jacket and jeans. From a knapsack he produced a wig of blond curls, a small makeup case, and a flashlight. In five more minutes, with Sheena's help, he looked astonishingly like Billy Angel.

"What do you think?" he asked. "Could I tour as the rock legend himself?"

"You probably have too much musical talent," she said.

He laughed. He was starting to like her.

"Listen," she said. "About this virus thing—"

"No time now," he said. "Billy Angel is due at the banquet."

"Please," she said, "at least summarize it. I'm risking my life here. I want to know for what."

"Okay," said Le Tour. "I don't really understand the details myself, but basically it's transmitted eyeball to eyeball, like some kind of super-hypnosis. But to make it work, both the person transmitting it and the person receiving it have to be chemically altered."

"Chemically altered?" said Sheena. "How?"

"You ingest this stuff, called TEEX, T-E-E-X. I don't know what it stands for, but it's some kind of extremely sophisticated neurological agent—tasteless, odorless, easy to hide in food."

"Like the food at tonight's banquet," said Sheena.

"Very good!" Le Tour laughed.

"So what does this stuff, this . . ."

"TEEX," said Le Tour.

"Right, what does this TEEX do?"

"It permanently alters your brain chemistry," said Le Tour. "I couldn't begin to comprehend the mechanism— some *very* smart people developed this—but essentially it changes your brain so that it can be programmed to send and receive commands through your eyes. Forever."

"Jesus," said Sheena. "Who developed this?"

"Now *that's* something I can't tell you," said Le Tour.

"It would have to be somebody with a *lot* of money," said Sheena, thinking out loud. "Somebody who could pay for top researchers and keep them quiet . . . and it would have to be somebody who knew that all these world leaders would be in one pl—*Jesus.*"

Le Tour was looking at her.

"It's Phillip Bates," she said. "It's *Phillip fucking Bates you're working for.*"

"You *are* a clever girl," he said. He leaned over and gave her a genuinely affectionate kiss.

He felt genuine regret when he broke her neck.

Chapter Eight

DIGITAL PRONATION

by James W. Hall

"Master Bates?"

"I told you not to call me that!"

Phillip Bates was standing naked in the center of his room, staring up at the extraordinary version of himself projected on the virtual reality window. The digital Bates was swinging a driver, a magnificent, flawless stroke, an amalgam of Zamora's grip, Sprague's backswing, Ben Hogan's shoulder turn, and Rita's hip snap.

"Master Bates?"

Phillip Bates turned to Edna Zuckerman. His male appendage was in a state of high agitation. The sight of himself swinging that perfect stroke was the most sexually charged experience Phillip Bates had ever known.

"How many times do I have to ask you not to call me that?"

"Do you think," Edna said, "just for a moment or two you could hang a sheet over that thing?"

She nodded in the general direction of Bates's midriff.

"I'm excited," Bates said. "This is what happens."

"Looking at yourself gets you excited?"

"Looking at myself do that," he said.

He stared up at the wondrous spectacle. His tee shot sailing hot and straight down the center of the fairway. Four hundred yards. Forget Tiger Woods. Forget Palmer and Nicklaus. Phillip Bates was the man to be reckoned with now. Phillip Bates could put that little white dimpled ball into cosmic orbit. He was going to make history. He was going to change the world as we know it.

"That isn't real, Master Bates. That's a bleeding illusion."

Phillip Bates drew his eyes from the virtual reality window and gave Edna a long smoldering look. On lesser mortals that same look had been known to permanently shrivel sphincter muscles, requiring a speedy surgical response.

"That, my dear Ms. Zuckerman, is the kind of uninformed, puerile judgment I've come to expect from you."

"But it's fake," she said. "It's just fucking electrons dancing on a screen."

"Name me something that isn't just electrons, Ms. Zuckerman. Go on, name one thing in the universe that isn't composed of the very same materials as that. But then you couldn't do that. Because there is nothing. And that's exactly my point. Now take another look at that. Look at that stroke, look at the fluid power, the effortlessness and grace. Tell me, have you ever seen such athletic splendor before? Such sublime, extraordinary elegance? No, you haven't. No one has. It has never existed before. Parts of that stroke have existed, yes. But not the stroke in its flawless entirety. And when the world sees that, when the world knows what Phillip Bates is capable of, my God, there'll be no stopping me."

"A golf swing's going to do that?"

"That's right, a golf swing."

"You're already the richest bleeding guy in the world."

"But you see, Edna, being rich is nothing. For money to mean something, for money to translate into a better world, that's the key. That's what greatness is made of."

"I repeat, a bleeding golf swing is going to do that?"

"Edna, Edna, Edna."

"You're a fucking onanist, that's what you are. Look at what you're bleeding doing. Abusing yourself with that golf glove for Christ sakes."

Phillip Bates looked down at his left hand, the white golf glove halted midstroke.

"I'm sorry," Bates said. "Was that impolite?"

"I'm a fucking lady," Edna said. "In case you bleeding forgot."

"This glove," Phillip Bates said, looking at the creamy material coating his left hand. "This is made from the hindquarters of old Democrats. Oh, I experimented with Republicans for a while, but their heinies were far too tough. Too much sitting around. Democrats are best. Very soft. The softest hide there is."

"How the hell did I get involved with you people?" Edna said. She was staring up at the digital Bates. Now he was chipping from the short rough, the ball sailing in a perfect arc, plonking on the green, then rolling to the lip of the cup, hanging for a second, then tumbling in.

"Down in two," Bates said. "An eagle."

"It's fake," Edna said. "And anyway, even if it were real, it would still be just fucking golf."

"God's game," Bates said.

Edna made a bleating noise of disdain. "Give me tennis any day," she said. "Now there's where you have your real athletes. You have to run, you have to sweat, you have to strike the ball in a split second and thread the needle past your fucking opponent. You have to be in shape to play good tennis. All you do in golf is stand around and watch your playing partners waggle their clubs. You sit in a golf cart, drink booze from a flask, and let a battery carry you up and down the slopes. Look at the bellies on golfers. You call them athletes? If you wanted to make a name for yourself as a bleeding jock, Master Bates, you should've taken up tennis. Golfers are about as athletic as fucking billiard players. Tossing darts is more aerobic."

Phillip Bates stripped off his golf glove and dropped it on the edge of his bed.

"Edna," he said calmly. "Do you have anything to report or are you here simply to unload each and every one of your uninformed opinions?" He held up a TV zapper and Edna watched as the window blinked off. Outside the glass wall it was dark and there were glistening ribbons of rain running across the pane. A normal window. Bates began to wilt.

Edna said, "They'll be starting the explosive sweep soon, Master Bates. For all the bleeding good it will do them."

Bates was staring wistfully at the darkened virtual

reality window. He seemed to have shrunken back into his gnomish body now. "Anything else?" he said.

Edna sat down on the edge of Bates's double-king bed. The mattress was filled with something spongy. A water bed full of gel? It moved beneath her butt like something alive, something cold and undulating, a reptilian presence. She popped to her feet.

"What the bleeding hell?"

Bates was still staring at the window. "I could be a great tennis player too," he said. "If I wanted, I could be Rocket Rod Laver. I could be Pancho Gonzales or Don Budge or Pete Sampras or John McEnroe or Borg. I could have them digitalized in no time and I could hit topspin and a twist serve. I could do all of that if I wanted."

"It'd still be a fucking hoax."

"Lew Hoad, Boris Becker, Andre Agassi."

"Le Tour has made the change," Edna said. "He's taken over Billy Angel's persona. He wanted you to know."

"Good," said Bates, still distracted by the tennis idea.

"He said to tell you that everything is set with the banquet. The virus is in the fucking Jell-O. Though why you put it in the Jell-O is a mystery to me. Not everyone likes Jell-O."

"Cherry Jell-O with pineapple chunks," Bates said. "Of course they do. Everyone loves cherry Jell-O."

Edna gave the mattress another prod. It responded to her touch like some kind of slithering Gila monster waking from a drowse, a ripple of movement.

"So tell me, Master Bates, there's something I don't bleeding understand."

"Yes?" Phillip Bates was still staring at the darkened window having reveries of Wimbledon and Roland Garros. A serve that was unreturnable, groundstrokes of balletic grace, a blur at the net.

"You're going to digitally insert yourself in the golf match tomorrow, right?"

"That's correct."

"You're out there with the great ones and your virtual reality self is beating the hell out of everybody. I fucking understand that much. Because, yeah, you can tamper with the broadcast signal, what gets sent over the airwaves. You control the bleeding airwaves, sure, you and your computer whizbangs. But what about all the people here, all the fucking eyewitnesses? They're going to see how sloppy you play, what a bleeding fucking gawky nincompoop you actually are."

"The Jumbotron," Bates said. He was winning the final game at Wimbledon in his head, jumping the net to shake hands with his opponent. The queen was there. She was bowing to him. She was curtseying. She was touching the steel blade of a sword to his shoulders. Sir Bates. I now pronounce you . . . Or whatever the hell they said at the end of Wimbledon when you entered the history books forever.

"What about the Jumbotron?"

"The gallery will be watching the match on the Jumbotron. They'll see my digital self."

"No they won't. They'll be watching you, the real in-the-flesh ninny that you are."

"They may watch me briefly, but what they'll remember is the Jumbotron."

"What they'll see is that you've got a swing like a mongoose having a seizure."

"Reality only lasts a second," Bates said. "Instant replay is forever."

Edna was staring at the mattress. It was quivering, sending out strange carnal vibrations.

"What the hell is in this bleeding mattress, for fuck's sake?"

Phillip Bates was picturing Jim Courier and Patrick Rafter and Stan Smith and Roscoe Tanner. Maybe he'd made a mistake settling on golf. Maybe Edna was right. Look at Zamora and Rita Shaughnessy and the rest of that gang. They were awfully out of shape. Probably couldn't run up a flight of stairs without risking a stroke. It would only take his Virtual Reality Team a few days to work up a digitalized tennis Bates.

"I asked you what in fucking bleeding hell is this mattress stuffed with?"

"Oh that," Bates said. "Don't prod it too hard. That's Semtex."

Edna stepped back from the bed. "You hid that shit in your mattress? Why in bleeding fuck did you do that? If you ask me, I think somebody's been inserting their digits into your fucking brain. Sleeping on Semtex."

"That's only a small portion of it," he said. "The rest is buried out on the eighteenth fairway with a percussion cap for a trigger. My little test in randomness. About this time tomorrow someone will step on it and then we'll have some quite unfortunate death and dismemberment."

"You booby-trapped your own golf course?"

"Of course I did."

"But why?"

"Why do you think, Edna?"

"Not for the bleeding publicity. Don't tell me that."

"Of course it's for the publicity. A golf tournament with the most powerful people in the world in attendance will draw substantial media, sure. But a terrorist attack on that golf tournament, endangering the lives of every major player on the world stage, serious death and destruction, well, Edna, think about it. Weeks of free publicity. And what will they all be watching over and over and over?"

"Your fucking golf swing."

"Exactly."

Then the revelation flashed through him. A white blast of understanding. A nuclear shock wave brightening his brain. Though he never would have admitted it, Edna's sneers at golf had threatened him mightily. Yes, he had wavered there for a moment. But that was the nature of faith, Bates reminded himself. To test. To doubt. And from that, to renew.

"Tennis is shit," Bates said.

"What?"

"Tennis and baseball, football, soccer, they're all shit. They're boring, full of the great tedious monotony of endless repetition. A court, a diamond, a hundred-yard field. Every game played exactly like the last one because there are only a few strokes and one implement, a racket, a bat. And think of it, each course is laid out with the identical, rigid demarcations. Boxes. It's like playing a game inside a packing crate. That's stupid, Edna, stupid and dull and spiritually bereft."

Edna was staring at the naked man. His skin seemed

to be growing luminescent. There was an angelic shine in his eyes, a vague halo hovering around him like a hazy force field.

"While golf, on the other hand, is infinitely variable, the mirror of life itself. Every course is unique, every round of golf is distinct, unlike every other round. Different clubs, different strokes. The physical challenges are of an infinite variety. You have the great arcing, gravity-defying tee shots, you have the careful, precise irons from the fairway, you have the chips, the fades, the draws, the slices, the hooks, the cold toppings, pitches, wedges, run-ups, lob pitches, fat-iron shots, single-handed shots, shots from the knees, bunker shots, sandies, and putt chips.

"You have the subtle reads of the green, sensing the grain of the grass, the shape and slope and texture, the angle and degree of break. You have a thousand different types of rough, bad lies, good lies, impossible lies. Trees become monsters, rocks and sand and water are suddenly mythic in their threatening countenance.

"The beauty and terror and unforgiving brutality of the natural landscape rises before you. You are a warrior, alone with your narrow shaft, on a quest that is ultimately unrealizable. And you are always awash in the wild tumult of weather, the thousand different breezes that must constantly be factored in, the ever-changing light, the rain, the mist, the fog, the blinding sun, the pewter sky, or immaculate sapphire heavens. That's golf, Edna. Full of sublime and infinite hazards, sublime and infinite pleasures. Day after day after day, it's never the same. That's why it's the greatest game, God's game, the challenge beyond all challenges. The putt at the end of the world."

Awestruck, Edna Zuckerman stared at Phillip Bates's beatific smile. She felt the ripple of gooseflesh rise on her back. The man was radiant, launched beyond the gravitational forces of the earth, powered by his own pixilated malarky.

"Fucking A," she managed to say. "Fucking A."

While the rich and powerful and the merely famous gathered in their tuxedos and evening gowns to eat the Bates banquet, Billy Sprague played a round of golf in the dark. It was not just a shadowy night, but a complete, total, utter, absolute blackness. Billy Sprague was a blind man. He was standing on the lightless bottom of the sea.

There was a drizzling mist, the quiet drowse of a breeze. There were the stray chirps and tweeterings of birds, the cooing and rustling and rattling restlessness of the burrowing night creatures, but there was nothing to see. Not even the white ball at his feet caught the faintest gleam of moonlight or starlight. The ball was invisible. The course was invisible. Billy Sprague was invisible.

He was on the eighteenth fairway, on the edge of the right rough. Two hundred and eighty yards out from the pin. He couldn't see the flag. He couldn't see his hands before his face. He set his feet, lined up the shot, sending out the weird, sightless sonar he had just discovered that he was capable of, adjusting his feet an inch or two to the right, and with this new blindman's clarity, this telescopic X-ray vision, Billy Sprague drove his ball into the darkest, blackest, most impenetrable gloom he'd ever known.

It sailed away.

Every rustling died. The wind stilled, the owls held their breath. Insects in the grass ceased their ceaseless twitching. The ghostly shadows of the recently destroyed Scottish old-growth forest, those thousand-year-old trees that once rose from this hallowed ground, all sighed in cosmic unison. And far away, a hundred yards into the dark undersea night, Billy heard the plink and plonk of his ball landing and then trickling into the par-five hole. Down in two. Double eagle in the absolute dark. A stone-blind perfect, flawless shot. Hidden in the blackest of nights, Billy stood naked in the dark, his skin aflame, a majestic glow from within. Twenty-one under par.

Not Buddha or Jesus Christ or even Ben Hogan had ever shot a round that low. No living or dead human being had even dreamed of accomplishing such a feat. And Billy Sprague had done it in the absolute dark.

No one to verify it, no one to check his scorecard. And no need for any of that. For Billy knew with dead certainty that he could repeat the feat tomorrow and the day after and into the indefinite future. Nothing could deter him, nothing could ever disrupt the absolute calm, the utter certainty that possessed him now. He was in love and he had transcended the mortal plane. He was the golfer of all golfers. The new paradigm. He would never have to open his eyes again.

He drew the cool night air into his lungs and hefted his bag and set off across the damp grass. He loved Rita and he loved this game. He loved the dark. He loved his nakedness. Billy Sprague had played the ultimate round of golf. He'd done it blind, and in so doing he had changed the world as we know it. He had met and surpassed Earle Doc Toland's greatest wishes for him. My God, he'd creamed that little ball. Creamed it and creamed it again and lofted it with magical and unearthly precision into the tiny invisible holes hidden in the absolute dark.

And yet it was only humility he felt. The sober, quiet joy and modesty toward this exalted sport.

As he slid his seven-iron back in the bag, he heard their voices. People in the distance. A woman's shrill inflection. Instantly he recognized the whining voice. He had listened to that sniveling mewl for years. Daisy Sprague, his ghoulish ex-wife, come to haunt him on the most perfect night of his life.

"There's a naked guy out there playing golf."

Fernando Gaspara, El Puma, adjusted his night-vision goggles. The world was a green, fuzzy glow. And thirty yards away there was a naked man stalking up onto the green, bending over to retrieve his ball from the hole.

The four of them had just arrived at the castle and were wandering around in the damp cheerless cold trying to figure out how they were going to crash this party and display what a fearsome golf machine El Puma had once again become. At that moment they were plodding across the eighteenth fairway, shivering and complaining about the marshy dankness, the bog fog.

"Ah yes, those are most certainly the flanks and backside and butt and shapely posterior of the man you once loved." El Puma tucked the shirttails of his pink Ban-Lon shirt into his orange-and-black plaid Sansabelt slacks. Behind him in the dark was the Doctor, so pleased with the Spaniard's steely new swing that he'd given up his attempts to alter the man's sense of fashion. "Yes, Mrs. Sprague, that does appear to be your former husband," the Doctor said.

"My Billy?"

Bringing up the rear of their little entourage, Putt Fenno stumbled over his own feet. He'd been doing that ever since he'd put on those damn night-vision goggles. Couldn't see a freaking thing in them. The whole goddamn night was green, like he was lying facedown in the fairway.

"The pro at Squat Possum?" Putt Fenno said. "That loser?"

Daisy Sprague couldn't help herself. She cupped her hands around her mouth and called out into the dark night. She shouted her Billy's secret pet name.

"Doofus! Oh, Doofus!"

As she stepped forward through the wet grass, she felt something tug at her right shoe. She peered down, glimpsing through her night-vision goggles a small round button protruding from the grass. Just as she put her full weight on the unknown, triggerlike thing, suddenly the night bloomed a dazzling white around them.

Something very much like a mushroom cloud enveloped the four obnoxious interlopers, and the million million molecules that composed them were instantaneously minced and double minced and minced a few more times until every solid part of their earthly forms was converted to gas, and together the four of them rose in a noxious cloud, mingling with the fog and mist, the dense broth that passed for air in that part of the world, tainting it for a moment. And then they were gone.

"Did you hear that?" Billy Angel, who was actually Le Tour and working for Phillip Bates, asked.

"How could I not hear it?" said Rita Shaughnessy. "It was an explosion of the first magnitude."

Rita was unbuttoning the pearl snaps on her ecru blouse. She'd never had a rock star before. It was an itch she was ready to scratch.

"That explosion," Rita said, "it reminds me of an orgasm I once had."

"Well, for me," Angel/Le Tour said, "that explosion reminds me of the song I'm going to sing tonight to the assemblage of important media personalities and bigwig dignitaries. The pope, royalty, everyone who is anyone or has ever been anyone, or has ever heard of or seen anyone or read so much as a *People* magazine article about anyone, including Tammy Faye Bakker, that great golf redneck."

"Hey," Rita said. "I didn't come to your room for a serenade. I came for that margarita you promised. And a little male companionship, though I'm certainly hoping it's not too little."

"Here's my song," Billy Angel said. "I wrote it just now without the aid of either a sense of rhythm or a brain."

"Spare me," Rita said.

But he did not.

I think the sky is as big as a golf course.
And the white puffy clouds float like golf balls
Rolling rolling rolling rolling across the heavens
Up out of bunkers
Up out of the deep rough
Up out of bondage and servitude and dopitude
The balls loft into the sky, they fall and they roll
We are the champions of the world
We are the eye of the tiger of the world
Golf is rough, golf is bunk, golf is a hazard and a good
    walk
Through the manicured woods. Rolling, rolling,
    rolling, rawhide.

"You like it, Rita? I'm dedicating it to you."

"Rawhide?"

"It's an allusion to one of the great songs of my youth. Hell-bent for leather, wishing my gal was by my side."

Rita began to rebutton her blouse. She was pleased to discover that there were limits to her lechery. It came with the force of a religious revelation. Rita Shaughnessy actually was capable of some limited sexual discrimination.

"I see you're buttoning your blouse, Rita," said Le Tour, who was still masquerading successfully as Billy

Angel. "Am I to infer that you were not aroused by my ballad? Does this mean you will not be my groupie after all?"

Rita finished buttoning the blouse. Then she tucked it back into the waistband of her plaid skirt. She felt like a schoolgirl. Clean and chaste. She had made a liberating decision. She was free of licentiousness, no longer a slave to the heat in her loins. She had turned down a rock star. A blond rock star at that.

Billy Angel said, "I make a pretty mean margarita. One sip and you'll be buzzing for a week. You won't care if you hook or slice or top or cup. You've never been bombed, Rita, until you've been bombed by me."

Rita hesitated at the doorway, staring at Le Tour, who she continued to mistakenly believe was Billy Angel.

"Thanks, kiddo, but no. I think I'll pass."

"Oh, come now. Wouldn't you rather pass out, my dear? I make a mean one. A doozie."

Rita licked her lips. Though the heat in her loins had cooled, her thirst had not abated. "No," she said. "I've got other plans."

"Not that Possum Squat golfing pro. Please tell me you're not throwing me aside for that total washout, flop, and failure, that fizzle and dud."

"Billy Sprague," she said, "is twice the man you are."

"You walk out that door and you'll be sorry, lovely Rita meter maid. You'll be very very fuckin' sorry. I promise you that."

She blew a kiss and walked.

"They're not eating their Jell-O," Phillip Bates said to Marlon Brando, who sat across from him. "They have to eat their Jell-O. It doesn't work if they don't eat their Jell-O."

"Are you all right?" said Marlon. "Do you need help of some kind, a Heimlich maneuver perhaps? It's a good way to get the meat chunks loose."

"They have to eat the Jell-O. I thought everyone loved Jell-O."

"I believe this gathering is really more of a liver pâté crowd," said Marlon. "If you ask me, Jell-O's a little boorish."

"But they have to eat it. The whole thing falls apart if they don't eat their Jell-O. Somebody's got to make them do it."

"Perhaps you could pay them," Brando said. "Bribe them to clean their plates. It always worked for my mother."

"Master Bates?" It was Edna Zuckerman again. She was standing behind his chair looking very distressed.

"I asked you not to call me that."

"Master Bates, we have a little problem."

"They're not eating their Jell-O. Now *that's* a problem."

"Uh, no sir. This is a little more serious, I'm afraid. We must take immediate action or the fate of the world as we know it may be irrevocably altered."

"But that's what the Jell-O's for."

"Master Bates, if you'll just step outside for a moment."

Marlon Brando was stealing a slab of beef off Barbara Walters's plate as she engaged in a lively discussion with Prince Harry to her right.

"Master Bates, please! There's not much time. If we don't do something quickly, this entire structure, the golf project, and everyone in this castle will be obliterated."

"How quickly?" Master Bates said.

Edna took a furious look at her wristwatch.

"I'd say we only have a few pages left. Master Bates, please, if we don't do something in that amount of time, forget it. We're all doomed."

Chapter Nine

RIGHT INTO THE
HEART OF THE CUP
by James Crumley

When the three pounds of Semtex exploded along the eighteenth fairway, Sheena Cameron came out of her self-induced yoga coma, buried in a cairn of heather and gorse, salt grass and thistle, smelling, she thought, like a pretentious Celtic folk band. She had sensed the violence in Le Tour's fingers a millisecond before he tried to break her neck.

Fortunately, her grandmother had been a hippie. Aggie Cameron had followed any number of second-rate British rock bands to India and had come back to Scotland with three things: five keys of temple hash, a thorough schooling in yoga, and Sheena's mother. When the hash sold out, Aggie supported herself, her daughter, and eventually her granddaughter by faking death and disaster in auto-pedestrian accidents. Her daughter wasn't interested in following the family tradition—a bit of rebellion perhaps, or a more abiding interest in the sexual merits of mental concentration and joys of a physical agility verging on the truly double-jointed—but Sheena was an apt pupil of the big con. And amazingly limber in the sack too.

The broken neck–death coma was the most lucrative trick of all, but also the hardest. Sheena came out of her coma with a splitting headache and a seriously bad attitude, discarded the drying vegetation that covered her, then struggled slowly toward the lights of the women's locker room through the lashings of a rain-shot North Sea wind, dragging her left leg like Frankenstein's monster. It took an hour, but finally she found herself standing in the locker where Le Tour had stashed her Walther PPK/S, a notoriously inaccurate pistol except at very close range. Except in the hands of James Bond or Sheena Cameron. She fell into a deep but troubled sleep, clutching an ancient golf shoe to her chest as her system shut down in relief.

Sheena didn't know how long she had been in standby state, but her clothes were still soaked when she was awakened by the low crooning of a familiar song from an old-time American television program. "Rawhide." What the fuck? she thought in a Scottish accent. With a rush of warmth, Sheena suddenly remembered that her beloved granny had loved the actor who had played Gil Favor because his face was mostly plastic and he looked dead. Granny Aggie could identify with that. Sheena peeked through the locker door's louvers. Billy Angel was fixing his mascara at the mirror across the room. He had come into the ladies' loo because Sean Connery had driven him out of the men's with a giant two-handed claymore he had snatched from his golf bag, threatening to cut off Billy's curly head and shove it up his sissy bum.

"Rawhide, my fucking ass!" Sheena screamed as she burst from the locker and buried the spikes of the golf shoe heel into the back of Le Tour's head. He just had time to see her reflection in the mirror, turn white, and die, with no chance at all to appreciate her political rant. "Random violence is just fucking random violence, you moron, when it lacks political motive!" she shouted. "Scotland is for the Scots."

"Right on, lady!" a deep voice shouted through the vent between the locker rooms, but Sheena paid no attention. Had she known it was Sean Connery, Sheena would have done a Godzilla through the drywall and thrown herself on her knees in front of his kilt. She might be a terrorist but she was Scottish, after all, and a woman nonetheless.

She stashed Le Tour in an empty locker, then it was the work of only a few moments, a small batch of makeup and a wig, for Sheena to turn herself into a fairly credible if somewhat miniature version of Nancy Lopez. She stepped back into the locker, fell into the cadence of her breathing, and slept as innocently as a south Alabama redneck safely escaped from a family reunion.

The foursome assembled on the first tee the next morning consisted of Rita Shaughnessy, Billy Sprague, Alfonzo Zamora—with Hector at last pried from his cot—and Phillip Bates. In the deep gray light Rita and Billy, still in the throes of newfound love, sparkled like diamonds in the rough in spite of the wet, windy fog that always presages a Scottish storm. Zamora looked a bit like a badly hungover Mexican mole. He had fallen deeply into the tequila the night before and had forgotten to clean his contacts that morning, so from the inside they looked like a wino's pissy sunglasses. Bates acted like a teenager with only three dollars in a border-town whorehouse, rocking from foot to foot, hustling his nuts as if to make sure that nobody had stolen them, and grinning as sadly as an egg-sucking hound with yolk on his nose. They were surrounded by television crews and bodyguards and a small gallery that included Ned, Edna, and Thomas, still working undercover. Everyone carefully avoided looking at the fresh crater surrounded by ground-under-repair yellow tape where the eighteenth fairway had once stood.

But one of the television cameramen had his camera pointed up into a three-hundred-year-old oak just off the first tee box, a tree that seemed to be decorated for a druid festival, festooned with crows and ravens perched sullenly in the oak's sturdy branches bearing obvious bits of flesh and clothing. One of the ravens held Putt Fenno's gnarled left ear in its beak, his silver cowboy-boot earring clearly visible. As dim-sighted as he was, Zamora swore to himself that he recognized, dangling from a crow's wing, a bit of tattooed skin flapping in the stiff breeze from the inner thigh of the man who once had thrashed him with a bamboo rod for the constant jerk in his putting stroke. Rita suspected that El Puma's foreskin was suspended from the crow's arrogant beak. And Billy Sprague knew without a doubt that the bloody scrap of butt-floss panties stuck to the tree's bark had belonged to his wretched ex-wife. But he was too happy to think about it.

Phillip Bates, on the other hand, refused to look at the decorated tree. In fact, he rapped the offending camera-man smartly across the backs of his thighs with the handle of his driver. Once, Bates had secretly flown to Eagleho Sanctuary, Arkansas, for a lesson in caddy-flogging from the famous Dr. Golf, so he knew how to get the best effect from a short, compact swing. The cameraman leapt into the air as if shot, then whimpered delightfully.

Things had not gone well for Phillip the night before. Nobody ate the cherry Jell-O. Not even Marlon Brando, who at one point had farted so loudly that Charlton Heston had threatened to shotgun his sorry Method ass just as soon as street-sweepers were legal in Polynesia. Marlon didn't seem too worried. He farted again, even more methodically. Madonna stopped by long enough to complain.

"Hey, dude," she said, "I don't mind when I can smell it. Hell, I don't even mind when I can taste it. But when it burns my eyes, I'm going home."

And promptly did. Perhaps for the first time in her professional career.

Marlon left too, stumbling over the sleeping pope's red shoes on his way to his suite to order room service. The pope cursed in Polish so loudly he woke Bob Hope, who slept in a chair across from him. A crowd of Swiss Guards disguised as cardinals rushed to the pope's side, mini Uzis sweeping the crowd.

Barbara Walters tried to seduce Phillip Bates into an interview after the small international and religious inci-dent, wanting his side of the story. Bates offered her the Jell-O dish.

"I ate Jell-O with Ronald Reagan once." She smirked. "But I'd never do it again. Probably."

Castro and Qaddafi were discussing Marx when Fidel asked Mu'ammar why he wore dresses and eye shadow and couldn't seem to grow a beard. Mu'ammar had a screaming hissy fit during which he accused Fidel of being a faggot because of the cigar thing. During the resultant food fight, many bowls of Jell-O were spilled. Phillip Bates saw Margaret Thatcher, whom he secretly adored, with a cube of Jell-O wriggling on her spoon halfway to her mouth. But being a veteran of British politics, Mrs. Thatcher had seen all of the food fights a decent body could stand. So she put her spoon down and left the table as regal as a queen. Bates nearly wept.

That was the most organized part of the evening. Before the serious drinking began. The resultant events were too disgusting to describe.

Of course, later most of the Scottish wait staff had some Jell-O because it was free, but as a people they had a long history of aggressive disobedience, so the TEEX had no more effect on them than an English shotgun pointed at their heads.

Phillip Bates went to bed in his top-floor suite as depressed as he had been since he was seventeen and his mother caught him trying to bugger his favorite hamster. She had buried the hamster's body in her rose garden, thrashed Phillip with the shovel handle, then spent the rest of the weekend holding him in her lap, kissing his pimpled face and cooing apologies.

In spite of a long night of severe discipline, including three iced-champagne high colonics provided by a truly disgusted Edna Zuckerman, Bates woke up among twisted sheets damp with his tears, wrapped in the arms of a champagne hangover the size of a grizzly bear, thinking "golf, God's game" as if it were the resolution to all the painful memories of a painful life. If only he could hit the occasional good drive. Or a decent chip shot. Or a putt that didn't fall off the far side of the green.

"Change the bed," he mumbled to the Spanish maid. She placed a tray on his desk—tea as stout as Mel Gibson's attitude and scones as sweet and as lovely as Rachel Ward's legs. "Change the bed," he repeated as he cracked his shin on the four inches of steel plate beneath the forty-seven pounds of Semtex in the water bed, then stumbled to his desk, wondering once again why so many people he really admired—especially the Australians—refused his repeated invitations to the tournament. Even his mother had declined, muttering something about the abuse of small woolly animals, as if she suspected her son coveted the sleepy congress of koala bears.

"*Sí, señor,*" the maid answered sweetly.

"See what?" Bates growled, then hit the computer. The Jumbotron filled all the windows of Rathgarve with silent, shimmering images. April in Paris. Maybe, or prewar Savannah. Bates wasn't sure he cared. At least there was golf in his future.

"Why don't you break his arms and legs?" Ned Gorman whispered to Thomas Franklin on the verge of the first tee box. Franklin had disguised himself as one of the Spice

Girls, but Gorman didn't think the effect was successful. "*You* know where she was all night."

Franklin had no idea what Gorman was talking about. He presumed Edna had spent the night with this incompetent Yank. "Even if your late boss was a Nancy-boy, Gorman, you don't have to be a jerk," he answered. He had his hand at his crotch and was staring raptly at Rita's large and marvelous buttocks as she rocked on the edge of the tee box, smooth, sleek muscle encased tightly in a pair of white pants. "You couldn't put a pair of panties under those britches with a paint gun."

"You're a foul and inconstant beast, Thomas Franklin," Ned said, then huffed away, thinking that J. Edgar had probably worn that same little black dress with the hat and the short heels, and they probably had matched perfectly.

"You've got the honors, Miss Shaughnessy," Bates said in a surprisingly deep voice, roughened by Tattinger, bad memories, and despair. He almost sounded as if his adolescence was over. "Tee 'em high and let 'em fly," he said, then slumped nervously in front of the PC in his cart.

Rita's gnomish caddy, afraid to touch her hand for fear of a sudden and embarrassing sexual experience, tossed her one of the special gold-plated tournament balls. Rita looked at the ball, then at Bates, and tossed it back. "You mind if I use my own balls?" she asked pleasantly.

"If you can find them." Zamora chuckled as Rita's caddy, who, like most of the others, wore a kilt for the first time in his life, sniffed the ball as if it were her bicycle seat, the lenses of his Coke-bottle glasses immediately clouding with steam.

Billy Sprague's practice swing came so close to

Zamora's head that his hairspray shattered. A boyish cowlick waved in the wind and black curls dangled across his low forehead.

"Watch it, *Tonto*," Zamora said as surly as a teenager. "Unless you want a nine-iron embedded in your forehead."

"You're such a child. How much cash you got on hand?" Billy asked calmly.

"Quarter of a mil, you Possum Squat son of a bitch," Zamora said.

"Want to play for it?" Billy said. "I'll give you three strokes on the front side and four on the back."

Rita turned from her stance over the ball to flash a smile like a beam of sunlight at Billy. Hector shook his giant head as if it were stone.

"I'll own your skinny white ass," Zamora said, his dark eyes glittering with greed and laughter. "And when you're broke in Bumfuck, Kansas, I'll take Rita to Mexico and—"

"That's Ohio," Billy said.

"*Qué?*"

"That's Bumfuck, Ohio."

"Whatever."

"Gentlemen," Bates interrupted. "It doesn't seem to follow the tournament's spirit of international peace and economic cooperation to wager on something as pure as golf."

"You play the fucking stock market, you pure dipshit," Zamora said. "We'll play the golf."

Bates didn't say a word. Zamora stuck out his hand. Billy Sprague just looked at it until Zamora put it back into his pocket. Rita turned on her drive with a swoop as smooth as an eagle's dive.

The first hole on Bates's course was an uphill four-hundred-eighty-yard par-four with a slight dogleg right. Oaks the size of apartment houses blocked the right approach, and a series of bunkers as deep as an elephant graveyard blocked the left. The landing area was in the center of the bunkers and about the size of a small house's backyard and two hundred eighty yards away. Of course, the Semtex crater on the left didn't come into play, but it sure caught the eye. Rita's drive nestled like an egg into a basket right in the middle front of the landing area.

"After you," Billy Sprague said.

"No way," Zamora said. "Hit the ball, Gomer."

"Alphabetical order on the first tee, gentlemen," Bates said from his cart. "Except for me. I'm last no matter what."

Billy Sprague teed up one of the tournament balls and, almost as if he didn't even care, hit the ball twenty yards beyond Rita's.

"Nice shot," Zamora said, addressed his ball, then hit it directly into the ball washer. But he'd hit it pretty good. The ball rebounded into the Plexiglas shield of Bates's cart, then bounced madly across the fairway into the far end of the crater.

"Mulligan?" Billy said.

"The day I take a mulligan from you, hayseed, is the day I give up golf," Zamora said. "Ground under repair," he added. "Free drop."

Meantime, a commotion had arisen in the gallery, where Henry Kissinger, Al Gore—both all decked out in the same pink plaid knickers and matching sweaters and shirts—and Margaret Thatcher in a tweed skirt and sensible sweater, waited behind the tee. Bob Costas, trying to move into a tougher sport—politics—was trying to talk to Kissinger and Gore. Kissinger, who didn't know who Costas was, and Gore, who did, refused to talk to little Bobby.

Phillip Bates watched with a raised eyebrow, then turned to his teed-up ball and, with a stroke as jerky as a marionette's dance or an old liberal's version of the Mashed Potato, scuffed his drive about a hundred yards down the center of the fairway. Of course, it didn't matter. The small gallery was mostly watching the shouting match among the pinkish plaid, who squabbled like a flock of guinea hens. And what the viewers of the Jumbotron in the castle saw, transmitted by the miniaturized virtual reality suit built into Bates's clothes to the PC in the cart and then to the main console in the castle, where it was enhanced, was a Phillip Bates swing as fluid as Rita's and stronger than Billy's that carried to another landing area no bigger than a queen-size bed seventy yards beyond their balls.

The virtual Bates won the hole with a perfect flag-high wedge, followed by a fourteen-foot putt across two breaks for a birdie. The actual Zamora, blinking wildly to clean last night's tequila scum off his contacts, scrambled to a workingman's par while Billy and Rita made pars as casually as they made love. Nobody even noticed when the real Phillip Bates gave himself a six-footer for an eight.

The rest of the front nine went the same way. Billy and Rita cruised, giggling a lot, paying more attention to each other than the game, both making the turn three under, Zamora scrambling just to stay even, and Bates a virtual dream but an actual disaster. He'd taken to obviously cheating but still was twenty over. Zamora's contacts were so cloudy that the oak trees looked like large green rocks, the ball a faint gleam at his feet. He had to do something.

"Hector," Zamora whispered to his caddy as he dropped his contacts into his huge hand, "I forgot to clean these fucking things. You gotta hustle up to my room and clean them. You'll find the stuff in the nightstand."

"I don't know nothing about this shit, man."

"Then read the fucking instructions, dumb fuck."

Hector's stone forehead wrinkled as imperceptibly as the earth's crust does under the influence of continental drift. Names hurt him. "Who's gonna carry your clubs, boss? You ain't carried clubs in twenty-five years."

"I'll put them on the geek's cart," Zamora said quickly. "Now run, Hector. I'm running out of holes."

Hector paused for a moment, handed the bag to his boss, then lumbered away in dreadfully slow motion. Zamora stepped over to Bates's cart, slammed his bag into the carrier, then fastened the strap.

"What are you doing?" Bates squealed.

"My caddy," Zamora said. "He had a personal emergency."

"He had what?"

"We gonna play golf?" Zamora said, repeating St. Peter's line to God in the old joke, "or fuck around?"

Across the tee, Billy wrapped his arm around Rita's shoulders. She fit surprisingly snugly for such a large woman, and quite warmly for a woman who didn't want to be possessed. "You've changed," he said.

"So have you," she responded.

"You make it all right, lady."

"What's with the bet? You planning to go home broke?"

"I'm planning to go home with you," he said.

"You planning to bear down on the back nine, boy?" she asked with a smile so dazzling that caddies two holes away tripped over their erections.

"What do you think?"

"Press," she said.

"I don't think it's right to press with money you don't have."

"Press with my money," she said. "The little fart owns a controlling interest in a course up in the mountains outside Ruidoso, New Mexico. Great scenery, perfect weather, and the sweetest eighteen holes you've ever seen."

"What would we do with a golf course?"

"Be the happiest club pros in America," she said. "It's become increasingly clear that I can't handle the Tour without liberal doses of drugs, alcohol, and . . ." At this point, Rita paused and blushed, an emotion so unfamiliar she thought she'd suddenly been overcome by dengue fever. Billy, on the other hand, thought the blush made her look incredibly cute.

". . . and aimless, unsatisfying sex."

"Can you stand a press, Zamora!" Billy shouted across the tee box.

Zamora, who had never refused a bet in his life, answered without thinking. "You bet your skinny gringo ass," he said, "and how about pressing on her ass, too."

"That's not my style anymore," Rita answered softly.

Then, realizing that he couldn't even make out Sprague's face, Zamora hustled over to Rita's caddy, snatched the glasses off his face, and quickly placed them on his. It wasn't perfect, but, damn, it was better, so much better, in fact, that he felt like a new man and apologized to Rita.

"Sorry," Zamora said. "No problem."

Rita and Billy exchanged amazed looks. Bates angrily plowed the cart down the path, glanced over his shoulder at Zamora's bag as if it were a large, ugly backseat driver.

Back in Bates's room the Spanish maid had nearly finished draining the thick gel out of the water bed. She turned to the stack of distilled water she planned to replace it with and didn't notice the pencil-slim remote detonator slip into the drain tube. Maria was no fool, and not a terrorist either. She was just a good peasant girl with a better job than she'd ever dreamed possible. And out of the heat too. She hated the heat, loved the clotted Scottish skies, the cold rain that felt like a blessing on her face. As she had changed the damp sheets, it occurred to her that perhaps she should change the water. It felt thick and tired. Maybe it had gotten old. Everything else did. Except for her boss. His image on the room's windows looked as fresh and clean as a baby's smile.

As Hector shambled as fast as he could past the following foursome on the ninth tee, he wondered who the gray golfer might be. Al Gore had taken the occasional rain-drop and the gusting wind as an excuse to encase his pink plaid in the death pallor of a cheap gray plastic rain suit. Kissinger had pulled a hamstring trying to evade the odd little man with the microphone and the oddly unruffled hair. Mrs. Thatcher was playing solid bogey golf, perfectly happy that it had only taken two rounds fired at Bob Costas's feet from the Webley .455 she carried in her bag to get him to move away. Of course, at the sound of the shots, automatic-weapon actions slammed back all over the course, chambering rounds, followed by muffled cursing as the security details unloaded their pieces.

Ned, still heartbroken over what he presumed was Edna's reinvolvement with Thomas Franklin, needed some place to direct his anger, so he grabbed the giant Hector as he passed.

"Where you headed, partner?"

Zamora's contacts Frisbee'd into the air, tiny saucers gleaming briefly in the ashen light before they dove into the rough grass like kamikaze alien ships just as the storm broke with a burst of lightning and a clap of thunder like an explosion.

"I've got a wife in Homestead," Hector answered, "another in Tampico, and a third one growing *mota* outside of Mendocino. So I guess I'm going home, wher-ever they'll take me in."

"Some people have all the luck," Ned said, distracted by the sudden appearance of Edna's sturdy body revealed among the dark shadowed trunks of the oaks by a flash of lightning. He also swore he'd seen Thomas's lumpy form lurching toward her.

Then a wall of rain as thick as flying mud swept over

the course, felling fat ewes and unstable golfers alike in its wild wake. But Ned had his bearings and would not be deterred.

Another lightning bolt split a giant oak just off the tenth tee, then bounced off to scatter Zamora's clubs. The lead foursome would have fallen down if they could have.

"What should we do?" Bates squealed as soon as he could.

"Hold up a one-iron!" Zamora shouted through the rain. "Not even God can hit a one-iron!" He had survived a direct strike once before and always played well after a close call. He was happy.

"Jesus," Rita said quietly as she and Billy huddled under an umbrella, her marvelous breasts beautiful beneath the damp Ban-Lon. "That was close."

"I'm hard as the fifteenth at Augusta," Billy said, drawing her into the shelter of the shattered oak.

The rain was over almost as quickly as it began. The fat ewes scrambled to their feet more quickly than the golfers. They had been molested by men in kilts before. Ned had worked his way into the dark forest. Thomas was jumping up and down, shouting at Edna about political and personal betrayal when Ned stepped around a thick oak trunk and shot him in the back of the head with his 10mm Glock. It was a bit of overkill at that range. Most of Franklin's brain and a recognizable chunk of his nose lay at Edna's feet.

"What the fuck are you doing?" she said.

"Protecting myself," Ned said, hysterically calm. He'd never shot anything before, not even a ratty-ass gull, much less a man. Either he was breathing too much or not enough. "I guess. I didn't exactly think about it," he added. "I loved you, Edna, and you spent the night with him."

"What you don't know would fill a book, you idiot," she said, glancing down at what was left of Franklin. "Do you perchance have some plan in mind?"

"I don't know," Ned said, unable to get the picture of J. Edgar in drag out of his head. "I think perhaps I'll shoot you, then myself," he suggested.

"Great plan, you idiot."

"Just off the top of my head, you know."

"I think I've got something a bit better," Edna said. "Think Grand Cayman."

"Grand what?" he asked. "Giant reptile?"

"A three-acre cay, six-bedroom house, and a million dollars tax free," she said.

"I don't understand," Ned said.

Edna dug into her purse, pulled out papers, waving them at him. "A fake Canadian passport, title to the cay and the house, letter of credit. We can disappear, you fool, have a real life," she said as she moved toward him and stuffed the papers back into her purse. "Nobody trying to break your arms and legs, darling. I'll make you forget that pimple-butted geek the first night."

"But what about the FBI—" Ned started to say.

A tiny woman who looked like Nancy Lopez stepped from behind a tree and fired a round from a small pistol into Ned's head just behind the right ear.

"Fucking FBI, my ass!" she screamed.

Edna knew that golfers were crazy, but she couldn't think of a reason for Nancy Lopez to shoot Ned. Though Edna was glad she had saved her the trouble. Edna also didn't know Nancy was so tiny. Maybe television made her look larger—like they say, the camera always adds ten pounds—and maybe it also masked the thick Scottish accent.

"Why did you do that?" Edna asked.

"The rat-fuck was going to do you, luv," Sheena said calmly. "And I hate fucking Yanks. Particularly the FB-fucking-I. And, unless I'm misinformed, we work for the same man." She lifted her wig to show Edna something of her real self.

"Well, thank you. I think."

"That thing you said," Sheena said, "about the island. Is that true? You must be more important to Bates than me, luv."

Edna preened. "I arranged the whole scam with the Semtex. Kept the FBI on the wrong track. And I can't even begin to tell you the sort of personal services I had to perform. Let's just say that his mother was very fond of champagne and high colonics."

"Enemas?" Sheena said. "Poor child."

"Sympathy is harder to come by when you're involved."

"But that thing you said about the island?"

"Just blowing a little smoke up Neddy's ass," Edna said as she reached into her purse. "Just some old papers—"

Edna nearly had the 10mm Glock out of her purse by the time Sheena emptied the Walther's clip into her forehead. Edna died without another word. Sheena piled the three bodies into the rill where she'd earlier stashed Ox and Angus—good Scotsmen, true, but blinded by personal agendas—then she went through Edna's purse, pulled out the important papers, and gave Edna's fake Canadian passport picture a long look.

"I can do that," Sheena quietly said to herself, then

glanced at the pile of bodies and the circle of ravens circling above. "And after I do Mr. Bates, I could do with a vacation."

Sheena pulled a tiny laptop tuned to Phillip Bates's Jumbotron signal out of her backpack. But instead of a picture of the virtual Bates on the tenth tee, Sheena saw a touching shot of the actual naked Bates masturbating with a golf glove to a videotape of the Shark's collapse in the '96 Masters.

"I'll be doing you a favor, Master Bates," Sheena whispered as she jammed another clip into the Walther and shoved it into her bra holster. "You poor bastard." Then she quickly hacked into the Jumbotron. She couldn't block Bates's private file from being transmitted to the screens in the castle, but she could block the feed to the whole wide world. Sheena just wanted to kill the little bastard. She didn't want to humiliate him.

In the great hall of the castle, a small group finished brunch. Only Dan Quayle, Marlon Brando, and the limping pope seemed to notice that something weird had replaced the golf tournament being broadcast over the Jumbotron: Phillip Bates whacking off to golf.

"Thank God Sean Connery has left," murmured the pope in Polish, crossing himself, "and thank God that there will be no children."

"What's that man doing?" Quayle sincerely wanted to know.

"Working on his short game," Brando snorted. "'Cause that's the only game he's got."

Celebrity guests and Macrodyne employees stirred frantically like gulls over a garbage scow, then fled like rats as it sank.

After the storm, the sky cleared. The Scottish sun even came out. The sheep lay down, butt to butt for protection, and dried out. Some of them for the first time in their lives.

As the first foursome played the back nine, only Zamora, with his new glasses, seemed to notice that the rest of the course was oddly deserted. Even the television crews and security details seemed to have disappeared. He didn't care though. With his newfound sight, Alfonzo knew that *now* he could hustle golf the rest of his life. He had politely offered Rita's caddy a turn with the glasses, but the gnome declined happily. The caddy had used his newly recovered myopia to bump into Rita's hard and beautiful body a dozen times on each hole. Post-Calvinist jism poured from his body like arterial blood. The front of his kilt dripped like a junkie's nose. But neither Rita nor Billy noticed. The three-stroke encounter behind the oak tree had made them oblivious to anything outside of themselves. Rita's hair seemed naturally blond for the first time in years. Billy grinned like a possum in a persimmon tree.

And Phillip Bates? He was playing the best golf of his life. Surviving the lightning strike had focused him perfectly. Not once did he think of his business or his billion dollars, not of his odd mother, who was after all just another lonely old woman, and the media fools who treated him like an odd but interesting child. All that went out of his mind. Phillip was the club, the ball, and the hole. He was also very happy.

Zamora had a couple of strokes of bad luck. On the par-three thirteenth his seven-iron looked dead stiff. Until it hit the flagstick and bounced into a bunker as deep as a grave and about half as wide. His bogey against Billy's birdie cost him two of his four strokes. On the par-four sixteenth Zamora hit one of his classic three-wood fades two hundred forty yards into the elevated green. Just like him, though, it was a little fat and a little short. His ball buried itself so deeply into the side of a bunker guarding the front of the green that only the Z was visible. Zamora saved par with the best sand shot of a life filled with thousands of great sand shots. Then a fifty-foot lag putt that stopped six inches below the hole on the steeply sloped green. But Billy Sprague's tap-in for an eagle wiped out Zamora's last two strokes.

"You just got to love it," Billy said to Zamora on the seventeenth tee.

"What?" he asked suspiciously.

"The golf," Billy said, still grinning. "That was a great hole, man. You're a genius, Zamora. Nobody in the world can recover from bad luck like you."

"Thanks, amigo. You ain't playing too badly yourself." Being able to see had turned Zamora back into the affable goof he'd been in his younger days.

"It's a great fucking tournament, Mr. Bates," Billy said. Rita blushed again. Her caddy almost fainted. Billy repeated himself. "A *great* tournament."

"Yes," Rita said softly as if about to drift off into the Celtic twilight later. "Yes. And yes again. And again."

"A kick in the ass, man," Zamora said.

Bates was so overcome he couldn't speak. So they played golf.

On the eighteenth tee, Billy turned to Phillip Bates. "You've got the honors, Mr. Bates," he said.

"What?"

"You birdied that hole," Rita said. "We all had par."

"What?" Bates said as if they weren't speaking English. He had been so happy he had forgotten to keep score or even count strokes. "My pleasure," he said, thinking, Fuck my virtual self. Then he teed up and hit a perfectly good two-hundred-twenty-yard drive right into the fat middle of the fairway.

The eighteenth at Rathgarve was a fairly easy five-hundred-seventy-yard hole with a slight dogleg to the left around a Semtex crater into a large but rolling green. Zamora and Billy were on in two. Rita and Bates in three. Zamora's ball was fifteen feet left of the hole, pin high, dead straight. Billy's ball was next to Bates's, but slightly uphill of the hole with a small, steep little ridge between it and the pin, Rita's ball just over the ridge.

The few remaining golfers and their hairy-legged caddies, having heard about the bet in the way golf people always hear about bets, formed a small gallery around the green. Al Gore stood woodenly on the edge of the crowd, a gray ghost on a sunny day among his Secret Service agents. There seemed to be more of them, Bates thought. Another bunch around a tall man in a slouch hat and sunglasses. Nancy Lopez stood at the edge of the green. I thought she was taller, Bates mused.

Sheena had followed Bates from the eleventh tee. She hated golf almost as much as she hated Bates, but as she followed him from hole to hole as his game improved dramatically, she couldn't help but notice the change. Slowly the incarnation of evil became a silly schoolboy, all elbows and grins and aimless dance steps. To stiffen her resolve, Sheena occasionally touched the Walther sheathed between her pert breasts, but she found her breath quickening and her heart pounding beneath her hand as Bates chipped in a thirty-footer to save par on the fourteenth as he rolled in a real character builder of a six-foot downhill putt on fifteen, then hit the green on sixteen with a seventy-yard sand wedge out of a fairway bunker.

Sheena didn't understand her reactions. Perhaps it was just the knowledge that she had only one more body to add to the pile before she could abandon murder forever. Or maybe it was something else altogether.

"Looks like you got me, man," Billy Sprague said to Zamora as they stepped onto the green at eighteen.

"I gotcha."

"Let's throw our golf courses into the pot," Billy said.

What would I do with a golf course in Bumfuck, Ohio? was almost visible on Zamora's lips as he hesitated.

"Give me a stroke," Billy said, "and I'll let Mr. Bates putt it."

Nobody could resist a bet like that. "You're on, man."

Bates hesitated, then shook himself like a dog rising from a nap. Hell, he'd never blinked when making deals for ten times half a million dollars. And it was just golf, a game, not God, or metaphysics, or even Chinese arithmetic, which he'd mastered at nine. "If that's the way you want it."

"That's the way we want it, Mr. Bates," Billy said.

"It's our gift to you," Rita added.

Rita and Billy marked their balls. Bates leaned over his

ball, realized that his hands were trembling. Why the hell was this so important? he wondered, then stepped back briefly to glance behind him. Billy and Rita wanted Bates to make this putt. Not because of the bet. They just wanted the best for him. At the edge of the gallery, Margaret Thatcher and Nancy Lopez smiled at him. They wanted him to make this putt.

Phillip Bates considered the putt for another millisecond, then stroked it with a firm sensual softness. The gleaming white sphere rolled briskly up the small ridge, then broke smartly left into the heart of the cup with a clunk as solid as the sound of a rich man's diamond engagement ring into the palm of the cutest hatcheck girl.

Bates, dizzy with a wave of joy that swept over him like a tsunami, was jumping up and down madly, though he was not quite sure why. Nor was he sure why Mrs. Thatcher grabbed his hand in a brief but firm shake that made his heart kick like a magician's bunny. He also wasn't sure why Nancy Lopez was hugging him and jumping up and down with him, nor why she had a steel plate between her pert breasts.

"What a beautiful fucking man you are," she shouted into his ear while they were in the air. Bates was in love before he hit the ground.

"But I thought you were married, Nancy."

"Not Nancy," she said. "Monica Fairway," she added, using the name off Edna's fake passport.

Bates, his joy at this news boundless, stepped back to survey his new love. "You'll always be Nancy to me," he said, hugging himself in ecstasy.

Unfortunately, Phillip forgot that he had the radio detonator under his arm. Now all that remaining Semtex was about to drive its explosive force down through the rotten stones of the castle like hot ice picks through Havarti.

He glanced up. If the looming towers of Rathgarve Castle didn't topple onto the eighteenth green and crush them all, the accompanying shock wave would certainly finish the job. He'd meant to be far from ground zero when the explosion took place, only his virtual self at risk. His intention was that when the smoke cleared from the rubble covering every celebrity, every leader of note on the planet, only Phillip Bates would be left to lead the bereft masses. A wonderful plan it had all been, all right. But now that he'd finally accomplished something physical in his actual life and won the love of the most desirable woman who had ever drawn breath, look what he'd gone and done.

The world as he knew it was about to end.

Shit.

But nothing happened. Then, three hundred yards to the west, where his sewer system dumped illegally into a Highland lake, a mushroom cloud of water vapor exploded into the sunlight. The sun shattered into a million tiny rainbows. The gallery cheered into the rolling waves of the explosion.

"Fireworks in the daytime are always so boring," Bates said. He didn't get where he was because he wasn't quick off the mark. "I thought rainbows more appropriate," he added, wrapping his arm over Nancy's shoulder and gazing soulfully into her sea-green eyes. "Will you have dinner with me, Nancy?"

Sheena, not immune to the sympathetic power of love or the political clout of a marriage that would make her richer than the queen and a more effective friend of Scottish nationalism than her years as a terrorist had, nodded briskly.

"Just one thing," she said.

"Anything."

"Call me Monica."

"Absolutely," Bates answered.

"How did you know?" Zamora asked Billy Sprague.

"You just know," he said. "Sometimes you just know."

"You never knew before."

"I know," Billy admitted.

Rita tipped the gnomish caddy as he stood close enough to hump her leg. Then she slapped his face gently, saying, "You behave yourself, you little devil, or I'll spank your butt." He swooned almost into a faint, but Rita didn't notice as she followed Billy and Zamora over to Phillip Bates.

"Great course," Zamora said to him, "and a great round of golf."

"Come back anytime," Bates said, then added, "Oh, you lost the bet. I'm so sorry."

"Not a problem," Zamora said. "Win some, lose some.

You only have to win more than you lose. And not be afraid to play."

Bates hugged Sheena closer to his chest. "What do we do now, Mr. Sprague?"

"Usually, we go to the nineteenth hole," he said, "have a beer, then play it all over again."

"Play it again?"

"Tell stories," Billy said.

"Maybe even lies," Rita added.

"I've never done that," Bates admitted.

"Come with us, man. We'll teach you how."

And they walked arm in arm into the rainbow-bright sunset, not exactly understanding how or why they had saved the world. Might have something to do with love. Or games. Or maybe just a compact backswing.

Epilogue

CURSE OF THE NINETEENTH HOLE

by Anonymous

The two mackintosh-clad men, each bearing a shovel at the shoulder, trudged slowly through the windswept gorse, their progress impeded by the need to stop from time to time to readjust their hold on the heavy bag they dragged behind them. Nor did it help that they'd had to wait until the last group had come in from the course, leaving them precious little light to navigate by. There was a glorious wedding party at Rathgarve Castle—a double wedding party, actually—but they would not be taking part now, would they?

"Reminds me of a certain joke, you know?" said the one named Mungo as they paused to catch a breath.

"Which one is that?" replied Magnus wearily. He'd caddied forty years and had heard every joke there was. Still, there was always hope. He reached into his jacket for the flask of Wretched Feather he always carried there and helped himself to a nip.

"You know, the boys who come in late, dragging their dead mate. 'Oh it was horrible. All day long, hit the ball, drag Keddy, hit the ball, drag Keddy.'"

Magnus nodded. "I never saw the humor in that. Should have left Keddy there on the first tee where he had the heart attack. Slowed up play the whole way around, I expect."

Mungo stared at him. "It's a *joke*, man."

"Nothing funny about slow play," Magnus replied.

"Forget it," Mungo said, bending to take hold of the bag again. It was an oversize canvas club carrier with the papal crest embroidered on one side, not only the perfect size for what they were carrying, but a nod toward a proper burial as well, so long as the man inside had been Catholic, that is. "You want to take your end?" he called to Magnus, who was at his flask again.

Magnus grunted and finally bent to help. Another forty yards and they were over a hillock and out of sight of the green, the course, even the castle itself. The perfect burying place. They rolled the bag aside and began to dig by the light of the stars.

An hour or so passed before Mungo's shovel struck something solid and Magnus's a moment after that. "Solid rock," said Mungo. "Deep enough, then."

Magnus, however, was poking about the bottom of the pit with the point of his shovel. He brought an ancient Zippo out of his pocket and flicked it to life, knelt to examine something at his feet.

"What is it?" Mungo asked, feeling a bit spooked by the shadows that flickered about the walls of the pit.

Magnus brushed some dirt aside and glanced down at the intricate design of a pentangle cut into the top of what was unmistakably a sarcophagus.

Mungo felt a chill run up his spine. "What's a pentangle?" he murmured. "Moreover, what's a sarcophagus?"

Magnus stood, his face gray. "Bad luck is what it is," he replied. "It's my guess we've disturbed the cursed resting place of the devil's own, the Untouchable Earl of Shank, and you know what that means. Let's finish our business and be gone from here."

He reached above him then and yanked hard on one of the grips of the canvas bag. He pulled again and the thing gave way, tumbling into the pit with a thud that reverberated through the stone at their feet.

"Come on, now," Magnus said to Mungo. "Cup your hands together, give me a leg up out of here. I'll pull you along after me."

"Nothing doing," Mungo said. "Send *me* up first. I'll do the pulling after."

"For God's sakes, man," Magnus said. "I'm the elder. *I* should be the first one out —"

He broke off suddenly, for the odd rumble they'd felt had not entirely died away, and in fact was growing louder by the moment. They looked down to see the top of the sarcophagus glowing red beneath their feet, a demon's face visible now within the outline of the pentangle. The canvas bag had begun to writhe with a life of its own.

"Cup your hands," cried Mungo.

"You first," cried Magnus back.

"Idiots," cried François Le Tour, as his revivified form burst from the canvas. Zipper teeth flew like molten filings about the pit.

Le Tour snatched Magnus by the throat with one arm and with the other caught a whimpering Mungo by the nape of the neck. He squeezed Magnus until the blood poured from his eyes and his ears, gave Mungo a shake that snapped his spine like a stick.

"Now," said Le Tour. He swatted at the golf cleats still embedded in the back of his skull and leapt to clutch the lip of the pit. His eyes were glowing red and tiny flames flickered where his nostrils flared. "Set another place at the table, children," he called in a voice that swept down toward the castle like a wolf's wail.

"You think you're going somewhere, do you?" came an answering voice from the darkness.

Le Tour glanced up. His hands—more like claws now—dug deeply into the earth at the lip of the pit, and he pulled his head up high for a better look. What he saw, illumined by the rising moon, made his lip curl into a sneer: a wrinkled old codger in a kilt and a Sunday bag with a single battered club slung across his frail shoulders.

"Squat Possum Toland," Le Tour said. "You're dead, old man."

"And so are you," answered Doc Toland. "I intend to see that you stay that way."

"I'll have you for dinner," Le Tour growled, scrabbling at the edge of the pit. In an instant he'd have his haunches beneath him, he'd spring to the old man's throat like El Puma going for the kill.

"There was never a shank left the face of this mashie," Toland said, whisking the club from his bag with a flourish that would have made Chi Chi Rodriguez blush.

Perfect backswing, pause at the top, downswing, and pronate, all in the blink of an eye. The silver club face seemed to grow huge as it snapped through the ghostly beams of the moon, and when the blade bit deep at its target, there came the sweetest sound in all of golf: Dead. Solid. Perfect.

Le Tour's head soared up, arcing high out over the firth like a blazing comet. Alfonzo Zamora, still agog with his new spectacles, was standing on a balcony of Rathgarve Castle with an all-is-forgiven arm about Hector's massive shoulders. They were the first to see it and call the alarm. Guests at the wedding of Phillip Bates and Monica Fairway would remark on the moment for years. And even Billy Sprague and Rita Shaughnessy, who were already otherwise indisposed, caught a glimpse of the blazing sight out a window of their honeymoon chamber.

"That's a good omen," Billy said, nestling his nose back where it belonged.

"Oh yes indeed," answered Rita, wrapping her arms about him.

And on they all went.

CONTRIBUTORS

LEE K. ABBOTT is a widely praised and often anthologized short story writer. His most recent collections include *Living after Midnight, Strangers in Paradise*, and *Love Is the Crooked Thing*.

DAVE BARRY's Pulitzer Prize–winning newspaper column appears in several hundred newspapers. His books include *Dave Barry Turns 50, Dave Barry's Guide to Guys*, and the recent *New York Times* best-selling novel *Big Trouble*.

RICHARD BAUSCH is the author of eight novels and four collections of stories. He is Heritage Professor of Writing at George Mason University. His most recent book is *Someone to Watch over Me: Stories* from HarperFlamingo, 1999.

JAMES CRUMLEY is the author of such critically acclaimed novels as *The Last Good Kiss*, *Dancing Bear*, *Bordersnakes*, and *The Mexican Tree Duck*, featuring over-the-edge detectives C. W. Sughrue and Milo Milodragovitch.

JAMES W. HALL is the national best-selling author of eleven highly praised crime/suspense novels including *Under Cover of Daylight*, *Buzz Cut*, *Body Language*, and, most recently, *Rough Draft*.

TAMI HOAG's most recent *New York Times* best-seller is *Ashes to Ashes*. Her titles, which total more than ten million copies in print, include *Thin Dark Line*, *Night Sins*, and *Guilty as Sin*.

TIM O'BRIEN won the National Book Award for *Going after Cacciato*. His two most recent novels, *Tomcat in Love* and *In the Lake of the Woods*, were both *New York Times* best-sellers.

RIDLEY PEARSON is the best-selling author of fifteen crime novels, including *Undercurrents*, *Probable Cause*, and *Beyond Recognition*. His latest novel, *Middle of Nowhere*, is to be published by Hyperion Books in early summer 2000. In 1990, he was the first American to be awarded the Raymond Chandler Fulbright Fellowship at Wadham College, Oxford University.

LES STANDIFORD is the national best-selling author of seven action/adventure novels, including *Spill*, *Presidential Deal*, and, most recently, *Black Mountain*. He directs the creative writing program at Florida International University.